Joe & Simone

Thank you for sharing the joy of our gifts of companion animals & the need to support the rescues who save those who need them.

Marty Richie

WITH HOPE THEY WAITED

With Hope They Waited

Marilyn Dickie

Copyright ©2013
Marilyn Dickie

All rights reserved. No part of this publication may be reproduced, stored in a retrieval system or transmitted in any form or by any means – electronic, mechanical, photocopying, and recording or otherwise – without the prior written permission of the author, except for brief passages quoted by a reviewer in a newspaper or magazine. To perform any of the above is an infringement of copyright law.

Note for Librarians: A cataloguing record for this book is available from Library and Archives Canada at www.collectionscanada.ca/amicus/index-e.html

ISBN – 978-1-77084-328-8

Printed in Canada
✿
on recycled paper

firstchoicebooks.ca
Victoria, BC

10 9 8 7 6 5 4 3 2

Dedication

This book is dedicated to animal rescue and its volunteers everywhere. The plight of these magical dogs at Mile 26 has opened my eyes, heart and mind with such respect, and to depths they have never been touched before.

To Catherine Baker Small, Anne Kennedy and Carla Davidson. They were, in that order, my first contacts of the Mile 26 rescue. They freely offered their friendship from the first day I inquired about the wonderful dog that now lays at my feet. They were in touch with me daily for over six months offering support, comfort and tons of laughter as I waited for the day when I could bring our chosen dog home. I value our friendship that continues to grow.

To Susan Elliott, I refer to her as the Mile 26 historian, and mom of two beautiful Mile 26 girls. Whenever I was stuck for certain information or who to call for what, Susan had or would find the answers. Your help, support, superb memory and friendship are very special to me.

To my dear friend, Kathy Jeanneault and her rescue called All Heart Pet Rescue. It was she, who never gave up on our dog, and for nine long months gave him exactly what he needed to become a part of the living again. In my heart, she will always be his very first human Mom and I thank you for entrusting him with our family. Kathy your unwavering dedication to the dogs who enter your gate in times of need is an inspiration to all. You have my 'furever' support and friendship.

To my husband Terry and daughter Cheryl. Thank you for your help, support and encouragement, to complete my dream. Thank you also for understanding and accepting my need to add yet one more four legged critter to our home. Thanks for sharing what is so dear to my heart, the needs of animals. Because you also have become involved with such enthusiasm, the joy brought to our lives and homes has become a very special gift to all of us.

And to my Dad, who lovingly taught me there is nothing that can be dreamed that can't be accomplished.

Some of the beautiful faces of Mile 26

Contents

Foreword - i

Acknowledgement – ii

Introduction - iv

Poem *'Whispers'* - v

Chapter One – *The Beginning* - 01

Chapter Two – *Calling All Angels* - 07

Chapter Three – *Help Arrives at Mile 26* - 11

Chapter Four – *Never Give Up* - 19

Chapter Five - *Mile 26 Volunteers*

Crystal Burkholder – 29

Anne Kennedy – 33

Carla Davidson – 41

Pamela Armstrong – 49

Poem *'Rescuers Are Angels'* - 53

Chapter Six – *Our Rescues*

Animal Rescue of Kapuskasing – 55

Northern Ontario Animal Welfare Society – 59

All Heart Pet Rescue – 63

Marnie Leach Volunteer - 71

Chapter Seven – *Calling Me Back, 'A Return to Mile 26'*

Poem *'Calling Me Back'* - 73

Chapter Eight – The Dogs *' Stories from the Mile 26 Families'*

Afterword - 209

Foreword

I went to Mile 26 to do a story about people. I was drawn by the story of Jean-Eudes, better known as the Dogman, and more specifically, the story of his son Ozzie, who rode up on the same train as me to help rescue the dogs his father had brought to the Northern wilderness.

Ozzie was compelled to go up, but not because the Dogman was his father, really more in despite of him. It was one thing they actually shared, the love of dogs. That inspired me to find a way to tell this story to the CBC listeners.

It was also a great radio story because of the other people who went up on the Polar Bear Express to Mile 26 that hot summer day. People who had given up their Saturday to tramp around in the bush, swarmed by mosquitos and tip-toe around piles of trash the Dogman collected and the ramshackle building where he lived just in hopes of giving a better life to an animal.

While my story was focused on the people, obviously the dogs were central characters as well. They made themselves known as soon as we got off the train that morning, taking long looks at us down the tracks and popping their heads out from behind trees and garbage piles as we wet the traps with moose meat.

I got to know them a lot better later in the day. I helped rescue volunteers carry some of the cages down the tracks to the boxcar where they had some food and water while waiting for the train to come back that night. I got growled at a little bit (but very little barking, which wasn't great for my radio piece, maybe the only dog story in CBC history without barking) and was nipped at once or twice. It was amazing to see how tenderly the volunteers treated these snarling dogs with matted fur and how quickly the feral attitude faded and you could see the first glimpses of the great pets these dogs would eventually become.

Now, with this book, this story becomes not about the Dogman but the dogs...and their new owners.

Erik White   CBC Radio Northeastern Ontario

Acknowledgements

How does one attempt to write a book they expect will draw the attention it needs to become a viable fundraiser for a cause near and dear to ones heart. I asked myself that question many times, finally realizing that there were dozens of families, volunteers and animal rescues, who shared that same want and need, are part of the Mile 26 family and had much to share in a book like this.

This particular animal rescue may not be a one of a kind to those in that field, but for the many families who became emotionally involved in the Mile 26 rescue, it will forever be remembered as one of the most unique and heartfelt endeavors that in the end gave us our magical dogs and an inspirational story to share.

Although this book shows only one author, it was in fact written by those who chose to be a part of the journey and offered their personal stories, photographs, facts about the rescue itself and information about their particular Animal Rescue facility and any part they had in the incredible journey of our dogs.

Therefore, credit should go where credit is due.

Firstly, huge thanks to every Mile 26 Family who shared with exuberance, very personal stories and photos of your special rescue dog and what he/she means to you. Your contributions and support over the many months to put this book together were the essential heart for its completion.

To the volunteers of the Mile 26 rescue, who put your personal lives on hold to brave the elements and save these dogs, there is no thank you big enough. To those who contributed a personal story and accounting of their own experience on this rescue for our book, a huge thank you.

To the rescues and shelters who provided transportation, medical care, a temporary home, rehabilitation, compassion and new beginnings for the dogs, mere words can never express the gratitude felt by every adoptive Mile 26 family.

'NOAWS' Northern Ontario Animal Welfare Society
'ARK' Animal Rescue of Kapuskasing
All Heart Pet Rescue
Moosonee Puppy Rescue
Pet Save Sudbury,
Clarington Animal Shelter
Timmins & District Humane Society
OSPCA

To those same rescues and shelters, who when asked to be a part of this book as a fundraiser for them, took the time to tell their story, submit photos and share information about their facility, to you come the donations raised by this book to assist continuation of the good work you do, along with an awesome thank you from the Mile 26 Families.

The **Ontario Northland Railway** offered free transportation daily to the rescue site for the volunteers and supplies, plus many of the crew took a personal approach in the saving of these dogs. Needless to say this rescue may not have happened without them. A much deserved debt of gratitude is owed to the ONR and we, the entire Mile 26 Family will never forget your kindness, as will the dogs never forget the sound of the train and the significance it played in their lives for so many years.

Several of the beautiful photographs in this book were taken and graciously contributed by Barb Dingwall. Thank you for sharing them and your gifted ability
to bring out the true beauty of these dogs.

Very special thanks to Denise Cochrane **'Power Design Portraits'** *https://www.facebook.com/PowerDesignPortraits* for her talented creation of the cover pages for each dogs chapter as well as many other illustrations which beautifully help interpret the story.

If anyone has been missed, please accept my sincerest apology. I trust that knowing because of your help, these lovely dogs were saved and have contributed bountiful joy and love to their new families is reward enough. Because of you, they are now able to say their own thank you by sharing their story of survival, thereby providing funding and awareness to save others like themselves.

Introduction

Inside the pages of this book you will find photographs of some very special dogs. You will follow their incredible journey from hopeless despair to safe and loving arms where a new life would begin.

Page by page you will read and see the true story of the dog rescue at Mile 26 in the summer of 2010. It was there, where over one hundred dogs and puppies lost their human caretaker in a disastrous fire that destroyed the only way of life they had known. His death left them to survive alone in the remote bush of northern Ontario where hunger and predators would surely bring them a swift and cruel end.

Included are personal accounts from those who braved the elements to save these dogs, giving you understanding of an animal rescue few others would undertake. Those volunteers were a dedicated team who endured the harshness of a remote area, where no roads exist. Follow these dogs and the heroes who saved them, down the lonely railroad track as one by one our heroes of rescue would take them to a world of new and foreign beginnings.

From there you will discover in each dogs own chapter, a very personal update through photographs and words from their adoptive families, how they have blossomed in their new life since the tragedy.

I have one of these magical dogs, his name is Rocky. Named Kahuna by his rescuers, he was my inspiration to put this book together and share the Mile 26 story with animal lovers and advocates everywhere. My dream is that by sharing this unique story, the book sales will raise much needed funding for the very rescues that saved these dogs and have also contributed their stories to the writing of this book. These funds will enable them to continue saving more animals in need of their help.

I also hope it will inspire many to personally join in the support of all aspects that assist animal rescue, fund shelters, help educate the public and promote decent animal welfare.

WHISPERS.....

We cannot hear your voices, we cannot feel your pain.
But deep inside our memories your story will remain.
A whisper down the track, a movement through the grass.
.. A shadow through the night sky like a lost soul of the past.
Along with you a human shadow, of a soul that cared for you.
He took you in when you needed him and tried to save the last few.
Your little lives so sweet, you eyes so full of love.
"Leave them they are wild" said the voices traveling from above.
But angels heard your voices...and angels they would come.
But no wings would bring them to you, lots of travel would have to be done.
They reached for you with love. They took you in their care.
They knew that they could never simply have been able to leave you there.
Your lives took on new meaning, as you traveled down that track.
The love that lay ahead, there would be no turning back.
Your story is ached within our hearts, but the story goes on forever.
As the survivors continue on path that has bought us all here together.
You came into our lives, many a story gone untold.
Now tenderly within our arms we will forever hold.

Denise Cochrane

Chapter One
The Beginning

No one really knows exactly when or why this large family of dogs began. We can only assume there was a strong desire in this human, who came to be known as The Dogman, to fill the needs of stray or unwanted dogs in and around his community. Out of respect for him and his family, I'll refer to him throughout the story simply as The Dogman of Mile 26. At the time of his death in May 2010, it was estimated that up to two hundred dogs of every size, age, breed & color shared his humble homestead in the bush, a half hour by train, north of Cochrane Ontario. It was there, where no access existed by road, plane or boat, and in the company of his canine friends, the Dogman lived his days without the simplest of modern conveniences.

The only means of travel to and from the closest town of Cochrane was to ride the rails of the Ontario Northland Railroad. This man had been an employee of the railroad for some years, and was well known by both current employees and the towns' people of Cochrane. In order to go to town for necessary supplies, he would hop the ONR's Polar Bear Express at the mile twenty six marker. His usual day to make the trip was a Tuesday, and he would return the following day. He was a familiar sight on the train and the streets of town, usually with a dog or two in tow, softly talking to himself and the dogs as he made his rounds. Word of mouth has it, that every penny of his pension income went to the feeding of his dogs. On his trips to town, he would also gather donations of food from local restaurants and other businesses. I was told that a few of the local farmers also helped out supplying vegetables, meat scraps and renderings. He was also given big tubs of grease or cooking oil on some of those trips and would often deep fry pots of potatoes for the dogs. One could often see him, with the help of ONR workers, loading carton after carton up into a boxcar, then he and all of his supplies would be dropped at the Mile 26 marker. Those familiar with these loads have said that they were often accompanied by very pungent odors too.

Although life for the Dogman, living away from the confines of acceptable social structure must have been serene and pleasurable, at times I feel it must also have been somewhat lonely with only the company of nature and his dogs. The harshness of the area, lack of every day convenience, extreme cold in winter plus the ever lurking danger of roaming bears would be too overwhelming for many. Add to this, the daily feeding, management and care of all of these dogs, one could imagine his days being very full leaving little time to pay much attention to his own personal needs. The Dogman did have family, but were estranged for many years. They did not share his enthusiasm for rescuing dogs. Over the years it appears the dogs took their place, with the exception of one child, regarding this ever growing family of dogs.

He lived in a cabin amongst the rubble of crumbling work sheds; old abandoned make shift buildings, and everywhere, piles of rotting debris. For the dogs, none of this mattered. They called it home, content to make their beds and find shelter with whatever they found on the grounds. This was where they played in the sunshine of summer, frolicked in the snow of winter and were fed. To this day, when I let my mind and imagination wander, I can picture them enjoying the lives and freedoms they had. I picture the adventures they would have shared when all was going well for them. They were a huge bonded family and had become survivors in their own secluded world. But then the reality of the darker side of things they also faced sets in. One man with a meager income could not possibly provide for the needs of this many dogs. They lacked nutritional food, medical care of any kind and for most of them; the only human interaction they knew was with their keeper, the Dogman of Mile 26. Many of these dogs in this wild and carefree life would have at some time been injured or become ill and passed away with none of the relief medical help could have provided. They were also constant prey for area predators, and exposed to the harshest conditions of all seasons.

As the years passed, the pack grew. It was not uncommon to see a dog tied to a pole or post at the train station in Cochrane on the days he made his trip to town for supplies. Everyone knew it would have been left there for the Dogman to take in. Few, if any of these dogs, would have been spayed or neutered, and despite the fact he only took females in the beginning, between wild packs seeking out mates and males being born, the numbers increased. It has been said that this man resorted to some desperate measures to keep the male dogs out and prevent the breeding, but in the end it became impossible. This meant an ongoing explosion of male hormones and an ever increasing population.

Life for the females was extremely difficult and draining. Many would become mothers while still just pups themselves, and without good nutrition the birthing and rearing of all these litters would take its toll.

Living as they did also left them very vulnerable to serious harm from predators. Bears, and feral dog packs were always lurking, ready to attack the nursing moms and helpless babies. It must have been exhausting to say the least, living on constant guard, with so much responsibility and in fear all of the time.

Several people in the area had complained to the OSPCA about the number of dogs he had in his care. It was obvious things were getting out of control and that this one man could not afford the costs of proper care for all these dogs. The cost of spaying and neutering even a few was not an option. The Ontario Northland Railroad was concerned too, as dogs were now running out onto the tracks knowing the train's sound usually meant their master's return and he would be coming to feed them. Reports were made to the OSPCA about dogs being hit by the passing trains, fearing it would only get worse as conditions continued to decline despite his best intentions to save the lives of these dogs. But sadly there was no help for the Dogman or his canine family, so the numbers and needs continued to grow even greater.

The Dogman of Mile 26 carried on the best way he could. He continued to take in the homeless and unwanted dogs, adding them to his ever growing pack. He continued his trips to town and continued to use all of his resources to feed and care for them. Some of the dogs shared his cabin with him, while others lived in the dilapidated shacks, or wherever they could find shelter from the elements.

Then the tragedy happened which ended his dreams and life as it was known to the dogs. On May 21, 2010 a nearby ONR work crew spotted him running in and out of his cabin, while all around him burned. A call went out to the authorities for help to fight the fire which had now started to spread to the nearby bush. As the fires burned, the chaos mounted with the arrival of water bombers attempting to extinguish those fires. Close to two hundred dogs were now being traumatized by fire and water bombs dropping on them from the sky. They could be seen everywhere, fleeing in terror for safety. Some remarkably did stay close to the immediate area. Mamas with their babies were so vulnerable now to injury or worse, death. One can only imagine the despair running through these petrified dogs as they experienced more frightening and foreign sights and sounds within hours, than they had been exposed to in their entire quiet lives in the bush.

After the blaze was extinguished, fire officials discovered the badly burned body of the Dogman of Mile 26, lying face down on the ground holding an armful of puppies. He must have been keeping new litters warm and safe inside his cabin and now he had died doing what he had done for more than thirty years, trying to save the dogs.

This is a photograph of the burned out cabin site. The dogs were slowly filtering back to find their master, his home, their family, their only refuge and means of survival. Little of what they knew was left and what was left was burnt black, soaked and smelling of smoke. It would be some time before others from the family would brave coming out from safe hiding places in the bush. Many would be cold, wet and totally terrified. Others could be badly injured, burned or even dead. The survivors had to stay together now, their protector was gone, but not the bears or packs of reported wild dogs. Their lives and entire future had changed in a matter of hours in that fire. Who was going to save them now? Who was going to care for the dogs?

Bears were hungry and roaming freely.

Chapter Two

Calling All Angels

Angel is the most accurate description I can think of for those involved in rescue of any kind. They are nothing less than heroes in my opinion, a breed of their own, particularly those who dedicate themselves to animal rescue. These special people are first to answer the call when and no matter where help is needed. Without a thought, they set aside personal plans and even family needs, to be out there on the front line. I'm sure the families of these people must have great compassion and understanding also. They are the personal support team behind every one in the field and deserve a huge amount of gratitude.

Word of the fire was spreading fast through local communities. From day one, many in that area involved in animal welfare, rescue and shelters were in constant touch with each other. They had contacted the Ministry of Natural Resources and the OSPCA to get as much information as possible on the probable condition and mental state of the dogs. The OSPCA had apparently already visited the area and deemed the dogs feral, there would be no rescue attempt by them and it was now an investigation. This rescue was going to be a real multi-faceted challenge. The dogs were in an isolated area, feral dogs and bears roamed free, there would be no protection from them or the weather should it turn bad. They needed volunteers who had been exposed to such conditions or at least pretty 'bush savvy' and not afraid to get involved in the worst case scenarios imaginable. Every possible situation had to be thought out and arranged for ahead of time but if any of the Mile 26 dogs were going to survive; help from these angels was needed quickly.

The Dogman had also been feeding the bears, perhaps to keep them happy and away from the dogs. They were already being sighted near the burned out cabin area looking for food. There was nothing standing between them and the dogs now and much to fear. The feral dogs were also closing in, putting all in peril, especially the pregnant or nursing moms and pups. The days were becoming very stressful for all of the dogs. They were grieving the loss of their master and possibly the loss of family if some of the dogs or pups had died in the fire. They would be very hungry, confused and tired by now, and the more depressed they became, the more weakness was seen by the stronger dogs of the pack. Were they now going to start turning on each other for survival? Time was running out. It had been over a week since the fire. When the dogs heard the train coming they would run out on the tracks to greet their master, only now the train didn't stop, and some were being hit. The trains just couldn't slow down in time to avoid them. Still, no one came to feed them; no one came to save them.

Back in civilization, volunteers, rescue and shelter owners and operators, were racing to get equipment and supplies together, packed up and ready to go. Arrangements were made with several shelters and rescues to be ready for incoming dogs. What a commitment on their part this was, they did not know the numbers or needs of the dogs that might be saved over the next days or weeks, yet their doors and arms were open to take in as many as each one could. The world of animal rescue is unique in that there are few questions asked when animals' lives are in danger. Other organizations as well as the public had come forward with donations of food, crates, collars, leashes, blankets, towels and so much more. They had no idea how many dogs they could capture, or what condition they would be in. They had been on their own now for almost 10 days. Some may have been badly injured by predators, the fire or the train and require immediate medical care, others could be quite feral or territorial and be a difficult catch. All would be stressed and fearful. The excitement and tension was peaking.

Plans were falling into place quickly now. Volunteers such as Moosonee Puppy Rescue were coming in from as far as Bracebridge ON. An Ontario Northland Railroad worker had been kind enough to take some video footage of some of the dogs and the area so they now had an idea of what it was like there. The ONR had also offered free transportation for volunteers and supplies to and from Cochrane daily and the use of a rail truck to move the captured dogs down the line to where transportation would be waiting. Without them, the dogs had no chance. The rail was the only way to reach them other than helicopter. They also had enough persons with their FAC and a firearm, as they would need one to go in with each rescue team for protection from the bears. They had divided themselves into teams of up to eight , and would be boarding the train in Cochrane around nine am, being dropped at the Mile 26 site around nine thirty am. The train would return some fourteen hours later and pick up the rescue team heading back to Cochrane. It would be dark, damp & rather eerie in the dense bush by that time of the night, for some very weary souls waiting for the train.

Help was on its way from all over. A chain of transport was already in motion. By crossing the Abitibi River by barge, they would drive up the tracks as close as they could get to Mile 26. There they would meet the rail truck carrying the rescued survivors, unload, assess, treat them if necessary, then re-crate and load them to be driven south to Cochrane, then off to the various rescues and shelters. The rescuers were now one day from loading on the train and heading to save the dogs. I doubt many got more than a few winks of sleep if any. The fear of the unknown plus the excitement of saving these precious souls must have surely made for a very restless night. For many of those boarding that train, it would also be a first meeting, as several had never met each other before this rescue. Some would have driven for hundreds of miles the day before and spent the night in Cochrane, others would make the drive from home if they could, meaning they would be on the road in the early morning hours to meet at the train station by seven am.

No turning back now, it was not an option, the dogs were waiting. I'm sure they knew help was coming, and wondering what was taking so long.

Chapter Three

Help Arrives at Mile 26

Ten days after the fire that took one mans life, destroying the only safe haven for more than one hundred terrified dogs; eight people boarded the Polar Bear Express. With hearts full of hope and a plan in place, they were on a mission to rescue as many of these unfortunate dogs as humanly possible.

Two of the rescue teams are shown here.

Mother Nature would not co-operate on that first day. It was a day of unrelenting cold northern winds and rain as the train stopped at Mile 26 and they unloaded their supplies of crates, food, blankets and all else needed for the task at hand. To everyone's surprise, they were suddenly surrounded by dozens of dogs, tails wagging and raising their voices as if in a song of "You're here at last."

Although they were relieved to see that some of the dogs were sociable, they knew the majority were hiding, obviously frightened and not sharing the same trust or social skills. And so, despite the miserable weather, it was time to get to work rounding up as many dogs as possible this first day. The coming weeks would prove to be filled with joys, frustrations, fear and every other emotion possible, but at this moment only one thing mattered, the dogs. The team began setting up

live traps and getting the crates organized to load and transport the social dogs who could be easily lured. Each dog was accounted for on paper, by sex, description and approximate age. Some who had distinctive looks or personality were given names or nick names.

They set up crates and supplies in an old box car to temporarily hold the captured dogs until they were sent down to the waiting transport crew. It also gave them a place to take a break now and then from the teaming rain and wind. Some of the live traps were set up near the burn site, as several of the dogs were staying in that area. Others were well camouflaged and set out further in the bush for the shy ones.

Although Mother Nature wasn't kind that day, luck sure was. The dogs were hungry; the social ones were curious and seemed happy they had some human attention again. I can only imagine the utter joy of those at the rescue that first day, as one by one; the live traps were being housed by yet another beautiful Mile 26 dog. The dogs would then be placed in a crate, and loaded in the box car. There the crate would be covered with a blanket and one of the team members stayed with them to keep them calm until there were enough to load on the ONR rail truck for the trip down the tracks to waiting arms and transportation.

It didn't take long to have enough dogs to send down those tracks. The teamwork was amazing and things were going very well. Now one by one the dogs were rolled down on a single track to where the rail truck would take them the rest of the way.

Those waiting for them were becoming very eager. They didn't know what to expect as far as the numbers or the conditions of the dogs. Would there be a few or a few dozen? Suddenly the rail truck appeared. There were eight dogs, sitting quite proud as they reached

another step on their journey. Not fire, bear attacks, feral dog packs and even death could mar the beauty and hope these brave dogs exuded. The Mile 26 dogs appeared magnificent and magical in every way.

As they unloaded the first rail truck, it was obvious these dogs had stayed strong in spirit, as if they knew without question rescue was coming for them. Although they must have been exhausted and unsure of all the strangers, many responded by wagging their tails as the volunteers spoke softly to them, comforting them and gaining their trust as they went along. Some co-operated reasonably well with having a collar and leash put on, others were reluctant to come out of the crate, but with kind encouragement, they all settled as they were offered some food and water. Another remarkable thing noticed by the volunteers was how well all of the dogs interacted with each other. They were calm, showing no aggression toward each other, even when they were offered food. It was obvious they were a very bonded pack, and even in this stressful situation showed their remarkable personalities.

The trailer being used to transport the dogs back to Cochrane would only hold eight crates, so after the dogs were fed, watered and given a bit of exercise, eight were loaded and sent on their way. More empty crates were returned on the truck back up to the rescue site. The first dogs rescued were the easy ones. They were calmer and seemed much more used to human interaction than those seen hiding in the bushes. Some were curious, constantly circling the area as if looking out for the others. Some were clearly terrified and simply hiding in fear.

The hours must have flown by that first day. So much to do, so much excitement of the unknown and the success of having been able to trap so many dogs. I try to imagine what it would have been like and how I might have reacted had I been there. It was cold, raining and there was not one familiar sight around them. There they were, dropped off in the middle of a bug infested nowhere with dozens of wild dogs not to mention the ever threatening presence of the bears.

Before long, seventeen more dogs were loaded on the rail truck and sent down the line to be transported to safety and shelter. This load carried mostly pups, some of which had been dug up from under rotted floors in the abandoned cabins. Due to the volunteers being well prepared, they were given puppy formula and despite being very frightened, calmed greatly once they were fed, warm and dry.

There are so many stories I could tell you about how, when and where all these beautiful pups and dogs made their way into a new life, but coming up in the following chapters, there are some heartwarming stories and photographs from some of the rescuers themselves, who were there and had the thrill of such a wonderful hands on experience.

And so the first day at Mile 26 was coming to an end. One more rail truck was sent out carrying five more adult dogs. They were wet, tired and frightened, but that would change with the tender care provided on their journey. All of the dogs were loaded up and headed for new lives one step at a time. Today, these dogs would cross the Abitibi River by barge and then beyond by road to the rescues waiting to take them in. A grand total of thirty one dogs were saved this first day.

*T*he joy felt by the volunteers must have been overwhelming as they headed back on the Polar Bear Express. What an exhausting but exhilarating day at Mile 26.

As the train pulled in to the station at Cochrane that night, the tired, soaked and bug bitten volunteers wearily unloaded themselves and their gear along with one more wet, sleepy and last minute rescue dog that would not be left behind. As drained as they must have been, I'm sure their spirits were soaring much higher than they had been hours earlier when they headed out on their mission, knowing they would be doing it all again tomorrow.

Chapter Four

Never Give Up

For the next several weeks, additional rescue teams regularly boarded the Polar Bear Express heading up to Mile 26. They knew there were more dogs waiting, pregnant females and possibly new litters who desperately needed them. The biggest obstacle now, the remaining dogs were frightened and didn't know it was OK to trust these strangers in their space, very much unlike the few dozen who met the first team.

It was around this time that a Facebook Page was set up with the aim of providing information to the public about this on going rescue, help in fund raising to pay for the medical needs of the dogs and assist in finding forever new homes for them. They needed to raise at least $15,000.00 just to cover the cost of having the dogs spayed and neutered, not to mention additional medical care such as dental work. Some of the dogs' mouths were in terrible condition with broken teeth and infection, a few of the females had mammary issues that would require surgery as well. The 'Save The Dogs at Mile 26' Facebook site received international attention and the response was very encouraging in seeking a good future for these dogs. It also became a good place for the new adoptive families to keep in touch and discuss the progress of the dogs. Many of the new adoptions were also posted here, and it was comforting for those concerned, to be able to keep track of each dog through its journey.

The media had started to carry short pieces on the news with some video of the rescued dogs with shelter staff. This was certainly bringing much needed attention to the plight of these dogs, the organizations and the volunteers working so hard to save them. It attracted more volunteers to join the trips to Mile 26 and donations of much needed cash, equipment and food for the dogs.

And so throughout the months of June and July, the rescue teams daily hit the trail to capture the dogs. At some point, with all good intentions I'm sure, someone had dumped a load of meat for the dogs. As much as this kept them happy, it made them even more elusive to trap, as they no longer found it necessary to come close to what they feared in search of food. The bears however were becoming more aggressive in their search for food. They were destroying the traps to get at the meat inside, and went so far as to totally remove a window, frame and all from one of the old cabins to steal the meat from a trap set up inside.

One day, strange noises were heard coming from this crumbling cabin. Inside, under rotting floors covered in trash, a little pup later named Josie was found. The bears frequented these old shacks looking for prey. These volunteers wouldn't rest until they were sure all the pups had been found, wherever they were hiding.

This is one of the entries from Anne Kennedy's journal. She was one of the volunteers through June & July. *"Yesterday, a team of six ventured back to Mile 26 in yet another successful attempt to retrieve dogs. It was raining when we were dropped off at the boxcar. We set the traps and went back to the boxcar, soaked to the skin. We had to keep our eyes on two very persistent bears. Max and I checked the traps a couple of hours later, only to find the bears had turned one over and mangled it almost beyond repair. The second trap had been tripped – the bear had obviously gone in, eaten the food, and managed to back out again. We moved the traps closer to the tracks so we could watch them from the boxcar. Later that day, we were walking along the tracks to check the traps when a bear stepped out from the bushes about forty feet in front of us. We had to scurry into the trees and Max sent off a warning shot. That was nerve wracking. At the cabin site, I cannot describe the utter squalor of the buildings. There is at*

least a foot of moldy clothing and garbage covering every surface of these tumbledown buildings. Bears and other predators frequently enter looking for food and shelter. Lydia was in one of the shacks looking for dogs when she discovered there was a bear in there with her. We captured a dog in a live trap and returned to search for more. Lydia shone the flashlight underneath a most disgusting cot and saw a little Spaniel/Lab mix peering back at her. The dog was frozen in fear and the only way to get her out was to crawl commando style through the filth to retrieve the little soul who appeared completely catatonic. I returned home at 2:45 am weary and wet, but happy. This had been the most gripping experience and the teams are amazing. We will continue to go up to Mile 26 until no more dogs are seen. We don't want to leave any behind."

    A daunting task to say the least. I have been told that the dogs faces could be seen peering out from the bush everywhere. They were too terrified to come for help and too smart to be easily trapped. They had pathways all throughout the bush and would circle the volunteers all around the area but never come quite close enough to be captured.

One of the most difficult times each day, was when it was time to leave. They knew there were so many dogs that needed to be pulled from there in order to survive. Seeing the faces of so many every day, made it impossible to give up, without knowing every possible method had been implemented to accomplish that goal.

Every volunteer was so dedicated and determined to save these dogs.

There were days when the rescue teams would spend hour after hour in the most miserable environment attempting to catch these dogs. They would do every thing right, but the dogs would elude them, meaning a long trip home, heavy hearted and empty handed. The Ministry of Natural Resources gave them some posts with fencing so they could make a pen and perhaps try to sedate them with darts, but that failed. These times were so stressful for all concerned. The days when even just one dog was taken into safety were very rewarding and worth every hour it took. The very happy group in this photo is on their way back to Cochrane. It would be very late at night, but the enthusiasm is incredible as they celebrate the rescue of ten beautiful dogs that day. The dogs were now traveling back from Mile 26 on the train, so other volunteers would meet the train and transport the dogs to a boarding kennel for the night, then hopefully off to a rescue who could take them the next day.

Beautiful smiles from beautiful souls. Our angels of rescue heading home on the train late at night. Ten dogs saved this day!

Some of the precious dogs the day they were rescued. Many displayed the scarred faces and bodies showing the long endured harshness of their survival here in the exposed elements.

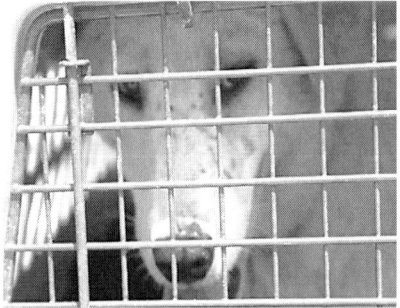

The photos on the previous two pages are just a few of the sixty-four beautiful souls brought out of the bush at Mile 26. At some point in August, an end to the rescue had to be called. Weather, predators and the fact that even after an overnight stay, no dogs had been sighted were the deciding factors. The last trip down those tracks must have brought forth so many strong emotions for the volunteers. Everyone involved knew for certain many were being left behind and it was heart breaking, but they had exhausted all means possible to save them. They were not about to be captured for whatever reasons. Some would be too fearful and unable to trust, others perhaps content with a chosen life of survival in the wild, yet others who were just destined to be left to nature.

A tear comes to my eye when I think of the ones left behind. For many months after the rescue ended, my sleep would be interrupted with visions of them, all on their own, perhaps peering down the tracks to see if anyone was coming back to visit. Where was the Dogman they trusted? The calm and quiet after the earlier horrific confusion they endured must have seemed almost odd. I still have dreams of this now and then, especially while writing this book, going though the photographs and the whole story in detail again. The emotions felt are almost like being there. Joy, anger, frustration, pride, hurt and amazement, all the feelings involved in any effort like this. When a halt must be called, and where 'enough' is difficult to accept as ever being enough, the many 'what ifs' haunt you for a very long time.

Along with the adults and pups being brought out of the bush, a new generation of Mile 26 dogs was also making its' journey to a new and more promising opportunity at life. Several pregnant females would safely carry these precious babies into a whole new world, soon to be born in the rescues and shelters and into the caring hands of kind people. Those same kind people would ensure a good and loving home would be found for each and every one of them. They were the ones who would benefit most from this rescue, as their start in this world would come with wonderful benefits like good nutrition, a warm place to lay their heads and a family to love and protect them. They would never know or feel the harsh realities of their parents' past lives and their struggle just to survive.

One of the litters born at Clarington Animal Shelter.

Chapter Five

A Few Words From Some of The Mile 26 Volunteers

When the dogs were brought back on the train into Cochrane each day, they needed a place to stay overnight before heading out to the various rescues. A lady named Crystal Burkholder owned a boarding and grooming facility called Finnegans in Cochrane. I asked Crystal if she could provide a little information on the general make up of Cochrane and her memories of the rescue and here is Crystal's contribution to the story.

Cochrane is a small community with a population of about 6,000 people. The town is quaint and picturesque with Lake Commando as it's' center. The lake being in the center of the community is often a gathering place for many community events such as 'Live Like a Northerner Summer Fest' and our long running winter carnival. Many people from Cochrane are outdoor enthusiasts no mater what Mother Nature tosses our way, whether it's -40 in the winter or +30 in the summer.

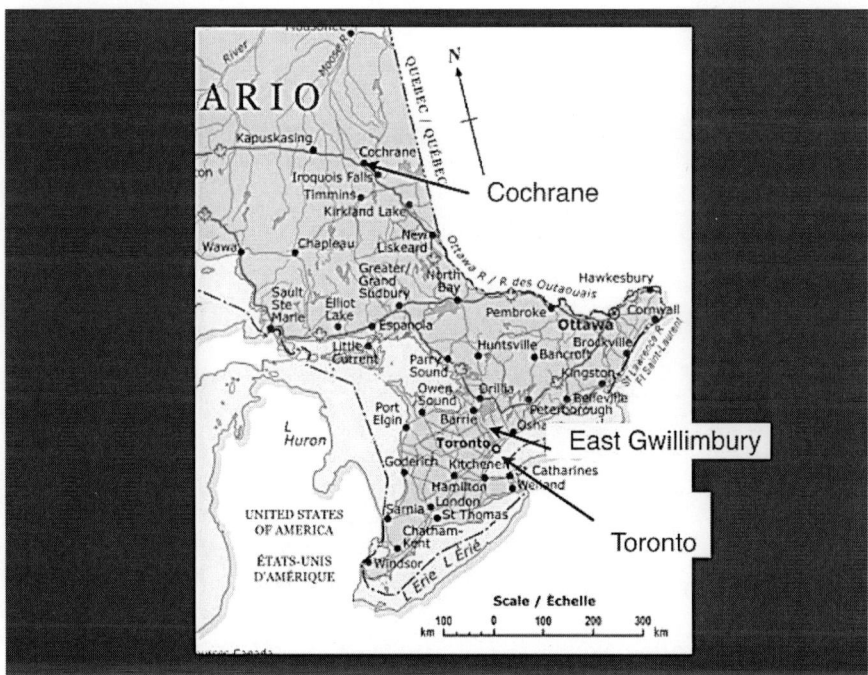

We enjoy many outdoor activities and sports such as hunting, fishing, camping, canoeing, kayaking, cross country skiing, snow machining, among others. Some of the industries in Cochrane include forestry with a number of small logging companies and two wood plants. Mining, with the re-opening of Detour Gold Mine, public sector, government, a number of small business owners and entrepreneurs, and the rail, which also has the popular tourist attraction, The Polar Bear Express, which offers a day excursion traveling 186 miles north to the edge of James Bay to Moosonee and Moose Factory.

Commando Lake

Mile 26 Recollection

In the spring of 2006, I was headed nowhere fast working in a position that didn't seem to show promise of advancement. At the same time, I had a cousin Rose, who was finishing up at high school and deciding where and what to take at college. After some deep consideration and conversations I decided to return and attend college with Rose, and take the Animal Grooming program at Northern College. The plan was, when we finished our program, Rose and I would open our own boarding kennel and grooming salon.

However, in the grand scheme of things, life would happen and plans change. Instead, I returned to Cochrane and with the encouragement of my family, bought my grandparents old home and began the process of renovating a bedroom to a grooming room as well as installing fences and converting the garage to a kennel.

In the spring of 2010, I remember being at my parent's house checking my Facebook and finding out about the fire in Wurtele, the horrible fate of Jean-Eudes and learning of all the now orphaned dogs. I kept a watchful eye on what was being organized, hoping I may be able to help somehow. I would liked to have been able to go on the 'rescue missions' to bring the dogs out; however with work, I just wasn't able to take the time off. After the first rescue trip, and hearing that the dogs had to spend the night in a trailer in town, I offered my kennel to house the next groups of rescued dogs., it was the least I could do. I had the space and a better set up to house the dogs in a more comfortable environment while shelters and foster homes were being arranged.

While in the kennel, the dogs had constant company from volunteers that came to feed and water, and just sit with the dogs trying to ease them out of their shell. Though I consider my contribution to the rescue of the Mile 26 dogs miniscule compared to the countless hours shelters and foster homes have spent rehabilitating and socializing the dogs, I am glad I was able to help and do my part on their journeys to their forever homes.

One of the most gratifying things about doing my part was, when I was camping with friends later that summer, unbeknown to me, I was camping with one of Jean-Eude's sisters, Ginette. After we became aware of whom each other was, I was thanked over and over for helping out her brothers dogs. Even now, over two years later, she still thanks me and is grateful to everyone who helped the dogs.

As for myself, I am still grooming and operating the boarding kennel. As of October, 2012, I am the new groomer at the local pet store, Cochrane Pet Services. Having a location up town in Cochrane will allow me to better serve the canine population (and their owners) of Cochrane. Finnegan's Boarding Kennel is still being run out of my home.

Crystal

Max and Anne Kennedy both made several trips up to Mile 26 in June & July of 2010. Anne is a member of Northern Ontario Animal Welfare Society (NOAWS). Here is her story of the incredible Mile 26 rescue.

I remember that day in June of 2010 as if it happened yesterday. I was sitting in my living room in Kirkland Lake watching the noon news, when suddenly a story came on that I became riveted to. Reports and film coverage taken at a location twenty-six miles north of Cochrane on the tracks between Cochrane and Moosonee, showing dogs everywhere, standing on the tracks in the rain, volunteers scrambling to live trap as many canine survivors as they could was being shown. I couldn't believe what I was seeing. I was glued to the television, listening intently to the story of how these dogs had become homeless from a tragic fire that had killed their caretaker on May 21st.

I quickly jotted down the name of an organization that was asking for any help available to save these dogs. Northern Ontario Animals Welfare Society was mentioned and I jumped to Google this group to offer any assistance I could. Something inside me drove me to contact this group of rescuers asking for help to save all these poor defenseless dogs. Rescuing animals was something I was not particularly experienced in, but I was hoping perhaps through some of my contacts with Helping Homeless Pets, there might be something I could do to help these poor homeless dogs.

I had no idea that my involvement in this incredible rescue would lead me on a path that would change my life forever, and bring me in contact with some of the most loving and caring people I could ever hope to meet. For me, Mile 26 has been the most positive influence and life changing event that I have ever experienced.

I started phoning everyone connected with the rescue, and after contacting Pam Armstrong of NOAWS, found out that rescue teams would be going up by train in a few days time. It was totally out of character for me to just show up at the train station with a bag of dog food, intent on being on that train to do whatever necessary to help save those dogs. But nothing could have kept me from doing this; it was something in my gut that pushed me with untold determination.

I enlisted the help of my husband Max, who has extensive experience in the bush, with packing my backpack. I had no idea what I might be facing. No one knew I was going, and to this day I still can't believe I actually showed up all alone, not knowing who I would be meeting or what I would be doing. All I could think of was getting those dogs to safety.

Early in the morning on June 17th I arrived all by myself at the train station in Cochrane with a large bag of dog food, and found other volunteers at the station. None of us knew each other, but we were all told to wait near the back of the train so we figured we were all there for the same reason. After a quick introduction, we all were given train tickets courtesy of the Ontario Northland Railway and we boarded the train in the early hours on that first of several trips to the burn site.

This trip was my first introduction to Carla Davidson. I immediately liked her and we connected on a deeper level of understanding and purpose and have been good friends ever since. We laughed on the way up as Carla told us all of how she had pilfered raw moose meat from her frig to bait the live traps and hadn't told her husband. Ozzie, the son of Jean Eudes, (the Dogman) told us that we would likely see dismembered dogs along the tracks when we arrived, and I really hoped that I wouldn't. He added that we should not look at all the dogs running around so as not to frighten them away.

We got off the train at Wurtele and thank God there were no dead dogs that I could see, there were however many running around the wheels of the train as it left for the rest of the journey to Moosonee.

Ozzie gave us a quick tour of the area and we set up our supplies in the boxcar provided for protection. (Erik White from CBC happened to be with us on this particular day.)

Everything was a learning experience, from how to set up a live trap to getting the trapped dogs into crates and safely into the boxcar.

We used whatever material we could find around the burn site, there were some very creative people in our group. We became a team, and by working together we trapped ten dogs that first day. It was incredibly exhilarating, I had found my niche. The camaraderie we shared would bond us all for a life in rescue. Driving home in the wee hours of the morning dirty, tired and bug bitten, I found myself happier than I had ever been in my life.

At the end of June, my husband Max joined our group of rescuers and we made several more trips into the bush, never failing to bring back at least a couple more dogs each trip.

Anne Kennedy

Max calming frightened Moe.

Repairing traps damaged by bears.

Max and Anne Kennedy have since moved to Englehart where they own & operate 'Kennedy's Howliday Pet Inn Resort' boarding facility.

Visit Kennedy's Howliday Pet Inn Resort on Facebook!

Kennedy's Howliday Pet Inn Resort
336352 Hwy # 11 Englehart ON P0J 1H0
705- 544-5477

Anne as an active volunteer member of the Northern Ontario Animal Welfare Society has for some time and still continues to assist with many fund raisers. She has also travelled to the far north native communities to help with spay/neuter clinics on the reserves. Together, Anne & Max have transported many a homeless animal for NOAWS and other rescues, to where they can find safety and the hope of their own forever homes. I know there will be many more pass through their door in the future.

*Since becoming acquainted thru the Mile 26 rescue, Anne has also become a very dear friend I am proud to call one of mine. I have to add a note she emailed to me one day when we were talking about the rescue.

"The audible, deep snoring that came from the boxcar after the dogs had settled while waiting for the train was a delight to hear. It was like they knew they were finally safe now. We should have tried to tape it.

The snoring was so loud sometimes it made us giggle. They were all so quiet once we finally got them. There was no frantic barking like you see in videos of puppy mill rescues, just this calm and serene energy of peace pervading the stillness of the bush. We often spoke in low tones and whispers so as not to disturb their slumber."

Two weary but now safe souls whose journeys have just begun.

Photos of Anne & Max at some fundraising events for NOAWS.

Kennedy family dogs at their Blessing. From the left: *Tia, Sunny and Lassie*

*C*arla Davidson made several trips to the Mile 26 rescue site in the summer of 2010. Carla also is a volunteer member of the Northern Ontario Animal Welfare Society. Here is her story of the rescue.

I will never forget where I was when I heard of the tragedy that occurred on May 21, 2010. There was a knock on my door at 9pm. It was my neighbor; she is my friend as well as a founding member of NOAWS. She asked "Have you heard what's happened?" Scores of dogs were left without their human, who had perished in a house fire.

She and I were leaving at 6 am to drive over an hour to catch the train at Cochrane which would bring us to Mile 26. At Mile 25, we started to see it. Dogs watching the train coming were running out of the bushes from everywhere. It was like a movie and I couldn't believe what I was seeing. This was not a populated area. There were no homes or cottages around; we were in the middle of absolutely nowhere. Yet the Dogman had lived here in a simple log cabin. These dogs were his family and were now orphaned.

We tried all day to gain the trust of these dogs, but none of them were interested. They were afraid and wanted nothing to do with us, so we left empty handed and heartbroken. We needed a plan 'B'. After much planning from many dedicated volunteers, we came up with three live traps. The Ontario Northland Railroad set up a boxcar so the rescuers had shelter from the elements and protection from the bears.

This would be our new home while at Mile 26. It was filled with dog food, about a dozen dog crates, water bottles, dog bowls and blankets. Throughout that summer, I would wake at 5 am, drive to Cochrane with my lunch and gear which included bear spray and a gun, then board the train with the team of the day.

Simon the bear loved to give us a rough time. She was getting used to us and decided she wanted the food in the traps herself. Even the shotgun blast didn't scare her at the end. I remember getting so angry with her that I grabbed a handful of rocks and started running after her, yelling and throwing the rocks. What was I thinking? I guess I felt that we had spent so much time together, that she wouldn't harm me. She didn't, but I also didn't do that again. Those poor traps were repaired often.

There was not a day during the rescue that I went home empty handed. We always managed to trap anywhere from one to ten dogs on the days I was there. I can't begin to describe the emotions I felt when we would go to a trap and see a new dog (most we had already named). The tears flowed on a regular basis. These poor dogs were so afraid, many smelled of skunk. They were hungry, scarred from fights and very, very tired.

Carla comforting a very weary Ella Blue.

So many of them lay down in the crates and just slept, as if to say "Finally I don't have to fight for my next meal." Some were so frightened they wouldn't eat or drink.

After sixty or so dogs were trapped, the Mile 26 story would not end, and it never will. We now have a Mile 26 Family which includes all of the lucky people who opened their homes and hearts to adopt one or more of these special dogs.

The Mile 26 rescue is a part of my life I will cherish forever. I live by the saying "Everything happens for a reason". These dogs steered my life into a direction that I never would have taken if it wasn't for them. I met some very special people who remain very good friends today.

Carla Davidson

To the Dogs of Mile 26, "I may have rescued you but in so many different ways you rescued me as well. Thank you. "

Offering comfort to the dogs while they wait in the boxcar.

Below, a visit with Mile 26 Little Anne in her new forever home. She will never forget Carla.

This calendar has become a treasured keepsake for many.

Carla has been a very active and long time volunteer member of NOAWS. Arranging and taking a personal interest in all areas of fund raising, she was instrumental in creating and getting the Mile 26 calendar together and out for sale to raise funds for the care of these dogs within months of their rescue. They were sold out in no time! She has such great energy partnered with a contagious smile and enviable motivational skills. Carla has also accompanied the vet teams to the far northern native communities to help with the spay/neuter clinics. On many occasions you will find her opening her home as an overnight pit stop for rescue dogs in transit or a litter of kittens that need homes. I am also very proud to call Carla a friend. She sat with my Mile 26 rescue dog in that old boxcar at Mile 26 and I'm so grateful to her for that. She was his first impression of human compassion and kindness in his new life. I can't think of any better example of that than through her.

*P*amela Armstrong is a long time, outstanding, dedicated member of the Northern Ontario Animal Welfare Society (NOAWS). I think it fair to say that without Pam and her determination, the Mile 26 rescue may not have taken place. She is a true inspiration to all involved in animal rescue. Here is what she had to say about her experience at Mile 26.

Save the dogs at Mile 26 happened because so many great people worked together. None of it would have happened without the help of compassionate, animal loving, and selfless people.

On May 21st, 2010 around 3:45pm, I received a call from Denice Bustrane in Moosonee asking me if I had heard about the fire in Wurtele. She told me the Dogman had died in the fire and was unsure of who would now take care of the dogs. Not sure what I was supposed to do with this information, I tried to contact the OSPCA to see if they could help. I was told the situation would be assessed and left it at that. On May 27th, a concerned ONR employee called me at home and asked what I was going to do for the dogs at Mile 26. Baffled, I began making calls. By late afternoon, NOAWS and other rescue groups were getting organized. We had no idea what to expect, we were getting reports of wild feral dogs and to make sure we brought guns. We had to make sure we went up with firearms just in case. We asked people for help by donating cages, food, leashes, collars, blankets, money and to volunteer their time.

By the following Monday morning my lawn had about forty cages on it. People labeled and left them for NOAWS to borrow. Food donations, collars, bowls and leashes were dropped off. Early Monday morning, a few Ontario Northland Railway workers came by my house and threw the supplies on a truck which was heading up the tracks.

I took a personal day from work and headed up the tracks with seven others. Heidi Pratt, Joanne Pretsel, Linda Byron-Fortin, Ozzie Levesque, Dina Chopp, Dean Peever and Randy Beauchamps jumped on the Polar Bear Express and headed to Mile 26 where we were greeted by approximately twenty-five dogs. We were able to trap many dogs right away as they were friendly and hungry. Once we had a full truck, we sent them down the tracks to Gardiner where we had people waiting to take some by road transport to Cochrane. Some of the first load went to Pups Moosonee Rescue in Bracebridge, others were sent to All Heart Pet Rescue in Powassan and ten remained at my house, housed in a trailer lent to us by Expedition Helicopter. The remaining ten went to Pet Save in Sudbury and ARK in Kapuskasing. The dogs we were not able to catch that first day were running back and forth over the tracks. Some of them were hiding but getting close enough to see us. I remember one we

named Carla Short Legs, breathing heavy and trembling in fear when we spotted her and a friend in the bush close to where the cabin was.

I went for a walk to a second cabin and I heard something. Randy and Ozzie had to tear the floorboards up to get at the puppies that were underneath. While on site we had to be careful not to venture off alone in case we ran into a bear. The site was polluted with garbage; there was even a freezer full of rotten meat. It was really hard to catch the dogs that were timid because it was such an open area. They had made trails all around the cabins. It was really neat because one minute you would see a dog at one end, then it would appear again on the totally opposite side. It was hard to even guess how many dogs were there, because this is how they travelled.

There were four dogs that we tried to catch that day but they were too scared. We had to leave them behind. Winkie was one of the dogs left

behind. She had a bad eye infection. Dina tried relentlessly to coax her into the cage, but she was too smart and too quick. As we pulled out that day, I saw a blonde long haired dog (now Bree) that came out on the tracks as the trucks were leaving. My heart broke. She looked so innocent, and she did not belong there in those woods.

When Bree was finally trapped, she was ready to burst and had her puppies shortly after the rescue.

The weeks that followed were stressful. We sent our vet team up to try and tranquilize a few of those that were impossible to trap. The Ministry of Natural Resources gave us some fencing and posts to make a penned in area to try darting them. This didn't work so we moved on to using the live traps borrowed from The North Bay Humane Society. Lydia Lefebvre came to the area to help organize the teams and go up the tracks. Volunteers were going up every other day trying to trap dogs. They would leave here at nine am and some days, not come out until midnight or later. I or other volunteers would meet the train and take the dogs to the boarding kennel where we would take them out and feed them in a small fenced in area. This was so challenging.

The dogs were super stressed. Most of them had never been on a leash in their lives. The ones they had to live trap had very little human contact and were very skittish. We housed them at Crystal Burkholder's Finnegan's Boarding and Grooming. We would not have been able to bring any more out without her help, we needed a place to temporarily house them until we could transport them to shelters equipped to take on these special dogs.

I was still working full time during all of this and caring for my two year old child. This busy two year old would come with me while I let these 'wild and feral' dogs out. Most of them just lacked trust and needed to be given love in order to trust again. We put out a plea for volunteers to take care of the dogs at the boarding kennel. This was so tough because some of the last dogs that came out of the bush did not even want to be touched. I would go there and have to dump some of them out of their kennels to go to the bathroom and then corral them back inside. The volunteers would sit inside with them, talking to them and trying to familiarize them with humans.

The Ontario Northland Railroad was so helpful and understanding during this rescue. They allowed us to travel the train at no cost until we got most of the dogs out. They even parked a boxcar at the site so our volunteers could store their stuff and have a safe place to go in case the bears came too close.

These dedicated volunteers returned to the site for six weeks until most of the dogs were gone. They spent long, sometimes very cold and wet days trying to get all of the dogs out. They would hang out in the boxcar to try and hide out from the flies, waiting for hours for the train to come back from Moosonee. The Ministry of Natural Resources were great also, and lent us a satellite phone so the crew could call in case of an emergency.

I must say, Mile 26 was an incredible experience for me. I met new people, learned new things, cried many tears, became a stronger person and did things I never thought I could do. NOAWS is a small group but it goes to show what can be done when people work together. I have so many to thank for their help in making this rescue possible.

Thank you to: Denice Bustrean, Heidi Pratt, Sharron Purdy, Paul Purdy, Lydia Lefebvre, Carla Davidson, Randy Deschamps, Joamme Pretsel, Lind Byron-Fortin, Ozzie Levesque, Dina Chopp, Dean Peever, Charlotte Sauvageau, Tina Lennon, Uli Huck, Nicole Porter, Alvin Porter, Kameryn Porter, Brysan Porter, Donna Paulin, Gen Byers, Patricia Morin, Expedition Helicopters, Crystal Burkholder (Finnegan's Boarding & Grooming) Anne Kennedy, Max Kennedy, Kathy Jeanneault (All Heart Pet Rescue), Jill Pessot (Pet Save), Lise Boulianne (ARK), Irene Landers, Lynn Michaud, Ontario Northland and their fantastic workers, everyone who donated cages, food and cash, and to my partner Silas, for his patience and understanding through yet another one of my stressful adventures.

Pam Armstrong

Chapter Six

Our Rescues

Mile 26 by Power Design Portraits

RESCUERS ARE ANGELS

Tail tucked between your legs,

Confusion in your eyes

I know it's hard to understand

That someone heard your cries.

When loneliness is all you know

And pain is all you feel

And no one can be trusted

And hunger's all too real.

That's the time the Lord sees you

And lets you know He's there

That's when He sends His messengers

The hearts that love and care.

Yes, rescuers are angels

You cannot see their wings

They keep them neatly folded

As they do their caring things.

The medicine to make you well,

Good food to make you strong.

And finally to help you learn

That hugs are never wrong.

The perfect place then must be found

The home where you can live,

Secure and safe and happy

With joy to get and give.

When you reach your Forever Home,

Your place to feel whole.

The angels smile and off they go

To save another soul.

   *Author Unknown*

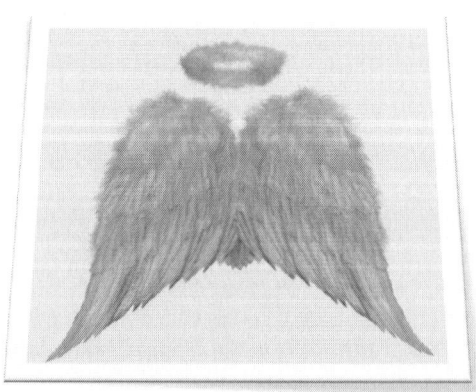

Animal Rescue of Kapuskasing has been in operation with the support of the Town of Kapuskasing since May of 2000. We have been rescuing, helping to rehome the needy pets we've accepted from Ogoki, Long Lac, Hornepayne, Hearst to Cochrane, Moose Factory & Moosonee, Kirkland Lake and New Liskeard.

What do we do?
Our mandate is to help animals. Neglected, abused or abandoned. We intervene when complaint calls are received, sometimes with the assistance of the OPP when warranted. We try to help ALL animals in distress. We also respond to calls from the OPP when pets are found in need. We've assisted the Women's' Shelter when help is needed to house a pet considered in possible danger in a domestic dispute.

Adoption program. To place pets in caring homes. Potential families are screened to make sure they are suitable candidates for a pet. We try to match the pet to the right family.

Education Programs. Media is used to inform the public with regards to pet welfare, pet care, and the importance of spaying and neutering.

Pet of The Week. Northern Times/Weekender/LeNord – We advertise fostered animals in need of new homes.

Pet Connect. We help the public find new families for pets they can no longer care for or want. We work with them but should not be thought of as a dumping station. We do not have a shelter to take in pets that already have owners.

Foster Homes. These are the backbone of our success. We operate without a housing shelter for our rescues. Foster homes are necessary to care for the animals in need. Vet care, food etc. is supplied by ARK.

Assist our local Veterinarians when they have animals for adoption.
Information Centre for the public needing pet info, etc.
Assist in finding lost/missing pets.
Assist with injured wildlife if needed.

Fundraising. We receive no funding or grants from any level of government, not even the OSPCA. The expenses of operating our Rescue

Group is funded by Private Donations (mailed or donation jars), Adoption Fees, Fundraising Activities e.g. Raffles, craft sales.

Our first priority is our local animals in need.

12 YRS. HELPING PETS IN NEED

Craft sale fund raiser.

On June 1, 2010 ARK drove to Cochrane and took in two Mile 26 rescue dogs named Blossom and Magik. Blossom was the most timid and nervous when they first arrived, but with the caring hand and patience of one of ARK's exceptional volunteer foster moms, Ghislaine Lemieux, they slowly changed and were lucky to be adopted together.

On June 25, 2010 three of Animal Rescue Kapuskasing's volunteers, Rachelle Hachey, Sarah Hachey and Louise Rosilius, headed out on the Polar Bear Express to Mile 26. Their team also had some volunteers from the OSPCA. This handsome fella was rescued that day. He was named Tex after one of the rescuers. Tex was adopted by a wonderful family, has gained a lot of trust and continues to thrive.

Our northern rescues along with dedicated volunteers continue to work with so little yet obtain outstanding results. They are often working with dogs and families in areas where little to no veterinary care is readily available. Life for our animals, especially the strays can be very harsh. Keeping good foster homes available is a challenge and finding volunteers to transport the animals to and from vet care, foster homes and often to their forever homes is an ongoing daily struggle. The animals lucky enough to come into their care are given everything they need to go on to new and rewarding lives. It's the volunteers and financial supporters who will keep our rescues strong. Please remember all rescues and the endless work they do. Visit ARK on Facebook!

Thank you ARK for all you do to make this world a better place for our animals in need.

Northern Ontario Animal Welfare Society

"For the Love of Animals"

WWW.NOAWS.COM

Northern Ontario Animal Welfare Society was founded in February, 1998. A non-profit group, dedicated to help solve the consequences of pet overpopulation in the communities of Iroquois Falls, Cochrane, Matheson and surrounding areas. We care for, neuter or spay, and find permanent homes for homeless animals.

NOAWS does not have a facility to shelter animals or any paid staff. We are run by volunteers who care for dogs and cats and foster them in their own homes and volunteers who fundraise to cover the expenses associated with the care of the animals and the programs we offer the communities.

Our Mission

1. To care for, neuter or spay and find homes for homeless animals.

2. To reduce pet overpopulation in Northern Ontario Communities by providing a spay/neuter subsidy program to low income families, individuals and senior citizens.

3. To educate the public regarding their pets and the importance of spaying/neutering, proper care and training, and the prevention of abuse.

4. To provide financial assistance to low income families, individuals and to senior citizens as it pertains to food, medical care, and assistance for their pets when funds allow.

Foster Home Program: Since our community has no animal shelter, NOAWS together with animal loving members of the community, care for abandoned animals until good permanent homes are found. Foster homes provide shelter, love and basic training to homeless animals while the shelter provides medical care, food and supplies (when funds are available). Donations of food and supplies are always needed, and sometimes provided by generous individuals or businesses. Because the costs associated with fostering must be covered by the organization, we are always in need of good foster homes, dog houses, litter boxes, etc.

Adoption Programs: The animals that are in the society's care are placed with responsible pet owners who offer a lifelong commitment to their.

animal companions, and who agree to neuter/spay the adopted pet if it has not already been done. Prospective owners answer an adoption questionnaire which enables the adoption coordinator to match new owners and homeless animals. No animal may be passed to another owner without the express permission of the Society. The Society also maintains a registry of animals for adoption, for members of the public who wish to place an animal up for adoption or who may be looking for a family pet.

Education Programs: Society members also visit schools, senior citizen residences and other local organizations to inform and respond to questions regarding animal welfare, pet care, spaying and neutering, etc.

Contact Information: Email - adoptions@noaws. com
Website – www.noaws.com

NOAWS and its volunteers were instrumental in the success of the Mile 26 Rescue. They worked with extreme tireless dedication both in the field, the after care of the dogs and on going fund raising for medical care. They have also assisted in raising funds and joining the medical spay/neuter teams to offer services in the far northern native communities. It is a goal to eliminate the problems and over population of abandoned street dogs whose lives are very harsh and short lived otherwise. With a dedicated spay/neuter program in place, these dogs will stand a chance at a better life.

If you follow them on Facebook, you will see the dedication and work never ceases as long as there is a need, they will answer the call. The fund raisers, requests for foster homes, and transporting of homeless pets across miles to those who can take them in, is a day like any other in the rescue world.

Please remember NOAWS and all animal rescues when ever and however you are able to contribute to the efforts and selfless work they do for our animals in need.

Northern Ontario Animal Welfare Society
Draw for Framed Paper Tole Picture
Created and Donated by Carolle Hannah

Get your Tickets at:
Paws and Claws in Timmins
Cochrane Pet Services
Iroquois Falls Animal Hospital
$2 Each Ticket
Draw Date: February 18th, 2013

Assorted fund raising events.

Every dollar matters!

Northern Ontario Animal Welfare Society (NOAWS)
Epicure **Fundraiser Open House**
@

Wed, January 23rd
From 11am to 2pm
135 Third St. W
Cochrane, ON
(705) 272-6701

Everyone is welcome!
Please visit www.rosannaulvstal.myepicure.com
or Needleworks for more information.

One of the most valuable contributions workers in animal rescue can provide is educating the public on responsible pet ownership and setting a good example. These photos were taken at one of the spay/neuter clinics NOAWS funded and assisted in at Kashechewan in 2012. They gave informative talks at the schools to offer the younger generation a better view of the humane and compassionate care their pets deserve. The main goal is to reduce the number of strays in these far northern communities and provide a better quality of life for the family pets.

The NOAWS volunteers assisting pre / post surgery, and comforting the dogs

All Heart Pet Rescue and Bear Creek Kennels have been in operation since 1997 under the ownership of Kathy Jeanneault. All heart is well known across Ontario for taking in unwanted dogs. We are an all breed rescue that takes in dogs in need from pounds all over Ontario, rehabilitating, training and re-homing them. Our favorite of all dogs is by far seniors.

In the past 16 years we have taken in dogs from Windsor, Sarnia, Belleville, Toronto, Whitby, London, Sudbury, New Liskeard, Moosonee, James Bay, Attiwapiskat, Kascheschewan, Fort Albany, Cochrane, Timmins, Huntsville, Perth, and Renfrew.

We have two shelter buildings that facilitate 30 dogs comfortably. We also have three large dog parks where the dogs spend a lot of time in the nice weather socializing and playing outside.

All Heart has built a strong and positive reputation with SPCA'S, rescue organizations and Vet clinics across Ontario as well as the residents of the communities it serves. Eighty percent of our intakes are dogs that are due to be euthanized if they aren't taken in.

We specialize in behavior modification such as biters, unsocial dogs, dominant dogs, and feral dogs as well. Our adoption success rate is ninety-nine percent each year.

All Heart is kept running by a large team of volunteers, donors and local merchants who, under the watchful eye of Kathy Jeanneault, ensure that dogs are matched with the perfect forever home. All Heart receives no government funding and relies on adoption fees and donations as well as a few key fundraisers to care for the dogs.

Open House every Sunday 12-3
430 Oakwood Road, Powassan ON
705-724-2630   www.ontariopetrescue.com
Facebook: All Heart Pet Rescue, Powassan ON

Every now and then we hear in the news about an event that involves a large number of dogs. Sometimes it's puppy mill raids or dog sledding outfits, others being about people passing away who owned far too many dogs.

In my opinion, the Dogman at Mile 26 had the best intentions to help any dog that crossed his path, but resources weren't plenty and the helping of dogs turned into an overload, as the dogs eventually bred among themselves and their offspring often unnoticed, were not socialized therefore becoming feral. (fe-ral 1. Esp of an animal, in a wild state, esp after escape from captivity or domestication: "a feral cat" 2. Resembling a wild animal)

Why do I call them feral? Even though they were fed meat by the man, a large majority of them were not approachable. These dogs were not vicious although their fighting instincts were in high gear. They had to fend for themselves and the survival of the fittest was what it became in this colony of dogs. Although I never visited the property, it wasn't hard to tell what the lifestyle of the man was.

When the first load of Mile 26 dogs arrived, their heads were bowed in their metal crates and their faces covered with many scars. They were being held hostage, away from their pack and being forced to be dependent on humans. Eye contact wasn't even considered by these dogs. Each dog was brought into a sixteen foot kennel run and all gates doubled locked as their fleeing instincts were high. After settling in for about a week, another small pack had been captured and delivered, bringing the total to thirteen Mile 26 dogs at All Heart. Oddly enough, there was a tale that the Dogman would destroy males to stop breeding, All Heart ended up with Tex, Kahuna, Dakota, Papa and Leggo. A few of the smaller dogs seemed to brighten up more quickly and I suspect that Abitibi, Nellie and Leggo may have been from the 'house pack'.

For days I would do nothing more than walk into the kennels, talk softly, lay down their food, clean and walk away. The dogs had to know they were safe, and handling them wasn't an option. I didn't want them to feel overwhelmed with people, but to merely observe that the hand that fed was the hand that loved. Barb Dingwall a graduate from the Vet Tech program also worked closely with me at All Heart that summer.

Within another week, the three 'assumed' house dogs of the Dogman were wiggling with joy when they saw us coming, others jammed as far into a corner as they could, heads down, tails tucked and clearly not wanting to be bothered. For many weeks, we never saw the dogs eat. They only ate at night when so one was around and when they felt safe to come out of their corner.

All of the dogs who came in are special to me, each with their own little quirks and progress. It is difficult to express what my heart feels about this venture and there aren't enough words to properly paint a picture of the event.

Albany: by far the alpha of the pack. A leader and confident, it was suspected she lived a good part of her life with someone before coming to Mile 26 as she had many more social skills than the others. Strong physical evidence of having had many many litters and many scars on her face no doubt from protecting all of her puppies.

Moonbeam: Very broken, she stayed with us for almost a year. Her confidence so low, lack of eye contact and no ability to show happiness or wag her tail.

Kahuna: (now Rocky) A boy with many scars inside and out. It was suspected that he was the father of many of the pups that were born after leaving Mile 26. Kahuna wasn't as fast to progress as some. Very reluctant to make eye contact or wag a tail. I will never forget the day after several months of baby steps; he finally made eye contact and took a few steps toward me. It was the beginning of a new life for that boy.

Kitchie: A silly pup that had it made. She wasn't scarred on the outside and still very trusting of all the dogs. Her social skills came very quickly as she was so young.

Nellie: What we thought to be Abitibi's mother. A wise, smaller dog, with many scars on her face, but more trusting of humans. We suspect she was a 'house pack' dog.

Abitibi: A sweet little girl, shy, but very receptive to human touch and love. Soon spoken for by Barb & sleeping under the covers with her.

Tex: Came to us after four months in a pound in Orangeville, he wasn't coming along and had to leave. Tex was suspected to be kin to Little Anne and Leggo. He was by far the most broken of all the dogs. He would try to crawl under his own skin when people approached him.

Dakota: A beautiful boy. Learned to trust people within six months or so and his progress much better than many, but his prey drive was high.

He and Papa were adopted by the same home but after about four months due to unforeseen circumstances, the dogs had to be given up and returned to All Heart. It was two years before he found his successful forever home.

Nipigon: A wonderful girl. Loving, shy, learned to trust and was wagging her tail within two months of constant care.

Papa: A very very battered boy. Scars all over his body and face from the many fights in his lifetime. Papa was shy for a very long time, staying with us for eighteen months. I'll always remember his two steps forward, one step back when he wanted a hand offered treat.

Winkie: The sweetest girl, missing one eye and goodness knows why. A soft girl who did better when surrounded with her pack mates. We think Winkie and Papa are related.

Leggo: Leggo had obviously suffered trauma in his life. Missing half of one front limb and part of his other front foot, didn't stop him from hobbling around and getting into mischief.

Gogama: My pride and joy. My angel who arrived with broken wings and left with wings that helped her fly to a better place. She was the only one of the Mile 26 dogs in my care that showed considerable aggression. She bared her teeth at anyone, so I was the only person to go in her kennel and push her to trust. I fed her daily as she shied away and bared her teeth, certainly telling me to back off, but I never did. I read up on dealing with feral, aggressive dogs, learning to sit in her kennel with my back to her. I would sit and sing or talk, and be confident and comfortable.

    After a few weeks, one of her injuries she had on arriving looked irritated. With heavy gloves, I cornered her, and while speaking in a soothing manner checked out the wound. The growling stopped; I removed my gloves and cleared the scabbing to let some pressure and the infection out. Almost immediately, she started to lick my hands, as if cleaning the wound for several minutes. After this moment, she watched for me, peering over her kennel to see where I was.

    From this, we progressed to brushing her matted hair and she nuzzled in to me. With a smile and eyes welled up with tears, my heart was filled with pure love. Gogama and I became such good friends. She would jump on me for love and hugs and kisses after those few days and it was wonderful.

Then one day it happened.....I was leaving the kennel. Gogama was out in the kennel yard to play with a few of the others and Barb was there at the rescue. I guess she didn't want me to leave without her and within a split second she wedged her head between a small gap between the fence and gate, a space too small to wiggle out of and she quickly passed away in the panic of it all. Within minutes poor Barb made the sad discovery. We were so torn and upset over this tragedy, and it took a very long time for Barb and me to recover from the pain of losing her, especially in this manner.

After all has been said and done, it is so important that the world knows about this rescue. I've seen a lot since I started rescue in 1995, but the Mile 26 was my most humbling rescue thus far. With these dogs, the progress, even the tiniest thing like a dog taking food from my hand or the wag of a tail meant we really were making a difference in their lives and they certainly have in mine. I still get updates from the adopters and have made friends that are like family.

Kathy Jeanneault

Nine Mile 26 dogs and families joined the fundraising All Heart Walk-a-thon in 2011.

All rescues depend on the public for both financial and emotional support. This was a most beautiful day with many supporters of All Heart. I'm so glad I got to be there with Rocky to join in the fund raising and meet other Mile 26-ers.

2011 All Heart Rescue walk.
Nine of 60+ Mile 26 dogs re-united for the first time on the anniversary of their rescue in 2010. Tex missing from photo :(

Together again at All Heart Pet Rescue's Annual Walk-a-Thon August 25, 2012
Twelve Mile 26'rs and proud family.
from left to right
Frankie, Papa, Dakota, Tex on Diane's left, Nellie, Kitchie, Rocky (Kahuna), Albany, Abitibi, Leggo, Little Anne, Tara

In 2012, twelve Mile 26 dogs and families, including my family, joined in the walk again. Many of our friends supported us with pledges. It was like a Mile 26 re-union and the dogs sure were excited to be together again. Some had been apart for over two years by this time. Seeing them together was such a joyful experience. I swear they were all smiling that day. Aside from the fun there was a lot of human emotion too. Wonder what 2013 will bring?

Even on the coldest days of winter, you're apt to find a half dozen Mile 26 dogs dropping by to say hello at All Heart. As I've said before, these dogs have brought such a wonderful family together, who would never have met and formed such friendships otherwise.

Up to three hundred or more dogs pass through the gates of All Heart Pet Rescue every year. Some with behavioral issues, others from good families who for some circumstance have no choice but to surrender them, others from neglect and abuse still others who were dumped at kill shelters simply because they were aging or their families just don't want them any more.

Mile 26 dogs, the early days.

A doggy Christmas Party held out in the big dog park. What a great day to mingle with other families of rescue dogs, socialize the pups and raise funds!

Come out to All Heart Pet Rescue any Sunday between noon and three pm. This is what you'll find, in the big dog park (well, not always snow). A fun place to visit and all of the adoptable dogs are available for you to socialize with. Everyone is welcomed to visit.

Please support your local rescues and shelters. The dogs depend on YOU!

Marnie Leach is a long time volunteer at All Heart Pet Rescue; these are her memories of the Mile 26 dogs taken in their care.

I began volunteering at All Heart in 2009. Being an animal lover, with two dogs and seven cats of my own, I wanted something I could do in my spare time to help animals. Over time, I became extremely close to the owner and Kathy became the sister I never had.

I vividly remember each of the dogs as they arrived, beginning around the first of June, 2010. They were in various shapes, sizes and dispositions. Some so withdrawn, others who adjusted into happy dogs very quickly. I spent a lot of time with Papa and Kahuna just talking softly, grooming and showing them it was OK to trust. The most awesome memory was when Papa placed his head on my lap for the first time so I could pet his head. The tears shed that day felt great!

As more time passed, I grew to love them all and all their funny little personalities. Being there every day, watching them transform into happy well adjusted dogs was so rewarding. Now all of them have their forever homes and receiving the lives they deserve with loving, warm families. I love hearing updates and seeing their new pictures. What's even better is when they visit and I see how happy they are, and to see me. I know they remember and are grateful for where they are today.

Out of all the dogs I have come in contact with, this group of Mile 26 dogs will always be in my heart. I will never forget the hardship they endured to get to us or the love and patience they accepted as we tried to help them. We were the lucky ones who got to help a pack of dogs fighting for their lives, journey to homes of their own, where they no longer have to fight for anything, most of all love.

To Abitibi, Albany, Winkie, Kitchie, Nellie, Dakota, Papa, Kahuna, Tex, Leggo, Moonbean & baby Moonshine, Nipagon and Gogama, you will always be a part of my heart.

Marnie Leach

Marnie doing what Marnie loves.

Chapter Seven

A Return to Mile 26

Calling Me Back

Today once more I will board that old train,
back to that place where I first shared your pain.
Back for the dogs that nature now claims,
back for those we left with no name.

For in the bush by that old railway track
sprits and memories lie...
Waiting for something, they know not what,
are lovingly calling me back.

Back to the day the fires burned,
causing panic, fear and dismay.
Back to the days, while in rescue we strove
to take a huge burden away.

Away from the souls of the innocents
who by now were so hungered and fearful.
Lovingly picked up and held with such hope,
many hours overwhelming and tearful.

White ones and black ones,
all colors in between.
Aged ones, young pups hidden in woodpiles
as they try to avoid being seen.

In they all went, some two by two.
mothers nursing babies, some with babies still due.
Up to the box car where soothing arms waited,
the power of love softly demonstrated.

Time is running out, what more can we do?
The bears are roaming, but can't we still save a few?
With regret we made our last trip down the track,
I whispered in leaving, "One day I'll be back."

I'll sit for awhile in familiar places,
remembering you all and your dear gentle faces.
I'll ask that some magic will tell you I'm hear,
with each gentle breeze I will feel you are near..

I'll leave some small tokens in memory of you,
and ask that you share them, with those we could save.
A great and kind spirit watches over you now,
every one, so loved, so beautiful and brave.

By Marilyn Dickie

Mile 26 marker along side the tracks where the journey began.

Early in the spring of 2011, a few of us Mile 26 moms were chatting on the Mile 26 Facebook page. By now, several of the families had gotten to know each other and were proudly posting photos and updates on a regular basis of our adopted four legged miracles. None of us have ever forgotten the dogs that had to be left behind when the rescue was finally ended. Now, approaching the first anniversary of that tragedy, the emotion was surfacing again. We also wondered if any dogs may have survived that first year alone. Anne Kennedy, who made several trips to the site during the rescue, said she had such a strong want to go back, and possibly find some closure by seeing the new green growth and life, where there had been such sadness and destruction.

As the conversation continued, the subject of a possible reunion of Mile 26 families came up. Wouldn't it be just wonderful if a few dozen of us could manage to come to a central location where we could have a big picnic or something and finally get to meet face to face? We imagined the joy of reuniting many of the dogs who had now been separated for almost a full year. This would not be easy as we live all over Ontario from the far north, east, and west and south. One family lives down in the Maritimes. The idea of meeting in Cochrane and taking the day ride thru Mile 26 on the Polar Bear Express came up and that was what we decided to strive for. We would try to do this as close as possible to May 21st, the anniversary of the Dogman's demise. We wanted to leave something at the Mile 26 marker for the public to see from the train, guaranteeing that the story of the Dogman and his would never be forgotten. Unfortunately, we just couldn't bring it together. Anne worked so hard to make this happen. She even got a discount on the rail tickets and offered her home for overnight guests but too many miles, conflicting days off of work, busy schedules and prior commitments existed to get this large group of veritable strangers, who were scattered across the whole province, in one place for one day.

Anne was determined to go as was Catherine Baker Small, who had adopted Little Anne from Mile 26. So, on July 17, 2011 Anne and Max Kennedy along with friends Deb and her daughter, Catherine and Gary Small with son James, Bryan MacMillan who adopted Mile 26 Nellie and Kitchie, Julie LeBelle Bernard and husband Mario, boarded the Polar

Bear Express. They took with them a lovely framed photo from the rescue and a beautiful wreath to leave at the site. The Ontario National Railroad had agreed to stop long enough at the Mile 26 marker to allow them (only a few persons) to depart the train and find a suitable place to leave the tokens of our remembrance.

Many of us who couldn't go had gathered on Facebook and were counting the hours of that morning, watching for a photo or posting from someone on the trip. The excitement and emotion surrounding this event was incredible. I can't say often enough that this rescue did much more than save 64 dogs along with the new generation of dogs that a number of mama dogs carried out with them. A magic came with them that united dozens of strangers and inspired a life changing direction in many of us. There are few I have spoken with during the writing of this book who don't agree that they feel somehow blessed by the effects of this rescue that will stay with us forever.

As the train was nearing Mile 26, the little group was greeted with an awesome and unexpected sight. There, looming above the bush was a

beautiful white cross someone had erected at the Mile 26 site. Try as we might, we still have no idea to this day who was responsible for it.

Finally, the train stopped and they made their way out into the bush where so many dogs had once roamed free. It was said they could be felt strongly in spirit that day and I believe it. I think, just as they knew help was coming after the fire, those left behind knew they weren't forgotten either. They expected we would return to confirm they too were just as special and loved as the lucky ones who were saved. Anne Kennedy commented "It's true; it was so serene, like all the spirits had gathered in respect. We only had a few minutes to do what we needed to do, but time stood still." Catherine Baker-Small stated, "It's still difficult to describe the feeling we all had while there. The silence was deafening yet defining, despite the huge diesel engine rumbling behind us. It seemed the whole world stopped for just a few minutes." The Mile 26 families will always consider these people the lucky few who got to go and say goodbye for all of us. Perhaps one day a few others, me included, will take that train ride too. I would love to take my special dog with me and sit quietly there for awhile to soak it all in. I'm sure Rocky would remember his old days.

James Small gathered a small sac of rocks from the site. We didn't know what the plan for them was, perhaps just a keepsake or a little memento for those who wanted one. Oddly, those stones are still together in that sac two years later, no one seems to feel good about separating them. It may sound foolish to some, but strangely enough, we all share the same feeling. One day we'll come up with an idea of what we should do with them.

Max, Anne and Catherine attaching the picture and wreath to the cross found there.

July 17, 2011

Anne said the sky that day reminded her of two hands holding a glowing heart.

And so the task was completed. We will all remember this day every year on May 21st, the actual anniversary date of the fire and again on July 17th, the date of this special trip back. We will no doubt continue to pull out the old photos, relive the many memories and shed a tear or two. Some of those who were at the rescue may feel differently. They may still question themselves and others, feeling they could have saved them all if only things had gone differently. I hope they know and understand how very proud we are of each one of them, for every dog's life they saved and all they accomplished. Few others would have even tried.

This was the view from the trains' window as they left. I hope several passengers have since asked and will continue to ask "What is the story that surrounds that big white cross out there?" This will keep the Mile 26 story alive and spreading even further. If you ever take that trip on the Polar Bear Express, travelling north from Cochrane, make sure you watch for the Mile 26 marker and remember this story of a very heart warming rescue and what it means to so many. The only thing missing will be the beautiful dogs running out to greet the train and their caregiver. If you should feel the slight wag of a tail against your leg or think you hear a faint happy bark in the distance, perhaps a few old souls are just saying hello. Their spirits will remain there forever.

Our Mile 26 rock collection. Thank you James for collecting them!

Forever remembered with love. R.I.P.

Chapter Eight

The Mile 26 Dogs and Their Stories

Bree

Bree's Story

The Amazing Rescue

I still remember the day, sitting on Pam's deck enjoying the warmth of the sun as it tried its best to warm the air after the winter months. I was excited for the long weekend as my husband and I were heading out to Mistango for our annual May Run party with friends.

Pam expressed her concern about an email received from Denice in Moosenee describing a horrible cabin fire that killed the man, leaving his many, many dogs homeless. Both Pam and Denice were very concerned for the well being of the dogs, I myself not giving it much thought as I didn't fully understand the dangers they faced. By Monday the anxiety was growing and Pam was contacting everyone for answers on who was going to rescue these dogs. With it being the May long weekend, she was not getting too far.

A week had now passed and Pam announced that she was putting a team together to go and see what they could do. The SPCA was not going to step in but any group willing to take on the task would not be discouraged from doing so. Here it all began, the 2010 Mile 26 dog rescue. Volunteers from all over the province had joined forces to lend a hand in whatever way they could.

With limited mobility from a herniated disc, I knew it was not in my best interest to join in the rescue, so stayed back on the receiving line. The first morning I saw the first group off at the train station, each one in adrenalin mode, excited about the unknown. I snapped a few photos, wishing I could go to take photos of every moment of this rescue.

We waited patiently for the first group to arrive. I had decided that my kids could miss school that day feeling they would learn much from the power of this group coming together to make this rescue happen. I was not wrong. Once they arrived, my nurturing instinct was so strong that I did not sense danger. The ladies around me brought to my attention that these dogs may not trust humans and possibly pose a level of danger, so I approached them slowly.

Heart Break

It wasn't long before I fell in love with a beautiful auburn spaniel mix. Named Shizzles at her foster home, we connected instantly. She rested her head on my legs as we sat on the ground, as I pet her while looking into her sad eyes, telling her time and time again that everything was going to be alright. My husband came by to meet the dogs and I introduced him to Shizzles, openly admitting to him that I thought we should give her a home. He was quick to snap me back into reality. We already had two dogs, live in town with no fenced yard, and were scheduled for a long vacation within five weeks time. Knowing he was right, I let my sensible side take over agreeing we just couldn't fit another dog into our busy lives. With my heart broken, I watched as Shizzles was loaded in the vehicle to be delivered to Pet Save Rescue in Sudbury to await her forever home. I vowed to get her if we achieved our dream of moving to the country should she still be waiting. Over the next few weeks there were many beautiful dogs I wanted to add to our family but my husband stood strong, forcing me to make that decision with my head, not my heart. I enjoyed the time I was blessed with, as each new group of dogs arrived.

Bree

Then we met Bree, a very pregnant, blonde collie mix who was the exact opposite of my childhood dog Mimi.

Same height, same face, eyes, temperament, but instead of midnight black, she was sun kissed blonde. I wanted to give her a home, but we were leaving for vacation in less than a week. I decided to leave it to fate saying to myself "if it's meant to be, it will be."

By the time we got back from vacation, Bree had her puppies and they were all being fostered in Timmins. I would ask Pam once in awhile of her status, but knew asking to see her was too much temptation to keep her, so I stayed away. It saddens me that I never got to see her puppies.

Now winter was on its way and the puppies were ready to move on, and were shipped south to the puppy rescue. Bree was scheduled for her spaying, and would finally have some peace and quiet in her new life, never to give birth again. I can only imagine how many of the dogs saved in that rescue were mothered by her.

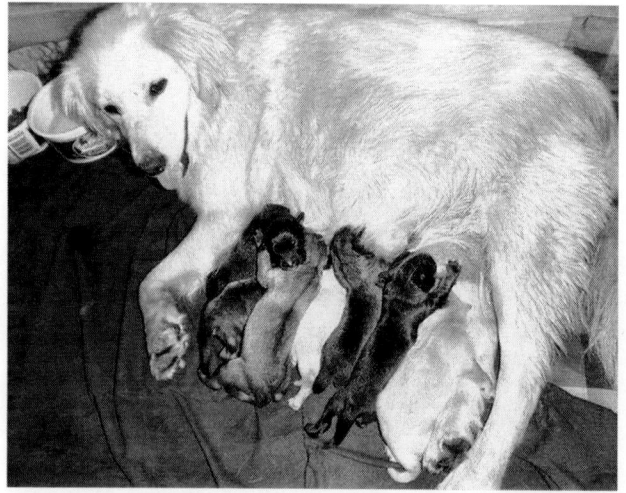

In early December 2010, a young couple from Cochrane emailed Pam about adopting a dog. They had their sights on Bree and within a few days, arrangements were made to move Bree to her new home, oddly enough, less than a block away from Pam's home. I was excited for her, but saddened that fate was not on my side, or was it?

Pam informed me that Bree's new family wasn't working out; she was a little too quiet for what they were looking for. Bree was homeless again. There was concern about getting her back to Timmins with our now daily snow storms. Jokingly, Pam asked if I wanted to foster Bree until after Christmas and was a bit shocked when I said "Yes, I would love to give Bree a home for the holidays!" (I already knew Bree was home with her forever family.)

Upon her arrival she was so timid and scared. The sadness in her eyes was just heartbreaking. It was obvious she couldn't grasp all the changes in her life. Where had all of her pack mates gone, why are there so many humans, so much noise and confusion? What was dangerous and what was safe, who or what can I trust or not trust in this new world? She was depressed, slept a lot and didn't even notice our cat Denzel. She had no understanding of this new and foreign world, how could I put her through it all again, by moving her to yet another home?

Love Conquers Fear

Our kids loved her instantly, but her feelings were not mutual to start. They made her feel nervous and with any fast movements Bree would shout out a warning. Kameryn, our daughter, being a dancer, often practiced her moves in the living room. It was during practice that we saw one of Bree's first warnings. She lunged at Kameryn without moving off the couch, while snarling and showing her teeth. Surprisingly it didn't scare Kameryn but made her feel concern for Bree. My oldest son Dyllan was home from school for the holidays, and quickly gave her the name Mr. Scruffles. The name didn't have much meaning as she was shaved bare of her beautiful fur and was a she not a he, but it was a name given by Dyllan and I found it rather cute.

The next warning came on Christmas eve. Bree was sleeping on the couch, trying to be invisible to the many people invited to share our Christmas eve celebrations. My nephew Tristen ran to give her a hug. Her first instinct was to lunge in warning but he was too close. Her tooth caught the inside of his nose causing it to bleed.

It wasn't her temperament but her fears shining through. We put her in in a quiet room for the rest of the evening, safe from the commotion.

She was slowly coming around and every now & then we'd get a glimpse of her true personality. By February, she was beginning to form a bond with our Husky dog Nikko. He is the most loveable fur baby you could meet. He loves the world and all in it. He too is a rescue dog from Kashechewan who made his way to our hearts just the year before. When Nikko would try to play with Bree, she would instantly submit to him, having no idea how to play.

Bree's biggest challenge was our older dog Myshia who had been rescued fro the streets of Cochrane eight years earlier. She is dominating with a strong personality and just wouldn't warm up to Bree. We spent many days scolding Myshia's bullying tactics, like standing between Bree and her food bowl. She would also growl warnings at Nikko for playing with her. Myshia's nose was out of sorts with her new fur baby.

The last of Bree's warnings came one night as she was lying on the floor. My youngest son Brysan went to hug her and she snarled a warning, coming very close to his face. I've seen it happen and this time it scared me, as my youngest sister was bitten by a dog when she was only three and been left with a scar on her left cheek. I quickly reacted by scolding Bree, telling her it was not OK to act like that. I tapped her nose and told her NO! She looked at me with that guilt stricken look we have all seen from a dog. This incident really scared me and I was worried that we would not be able to keep her. I feared perhaps she needed a home where there were no children, but the more we talked about it, the more certain I was that I was not ready to give up on her. We agreed to give her a little longer and are glad we did, as it turned out that was her last warning. I guess when I scolded her it made me the dominant leader.

Our Very Own Happy Ending

So here we are, all this in the past and we couldn't be happier with the outcome. She and Nikko are best friends and she now knows how to play like a puppy. They spend hours together curled up on the couch. Bree has adjusted fully to her new life with us. Although Myshia is still too grumpy to warm up to Bree, she has learned to tolerate her, like the mother of two wild and crazy pups, she keeps them in line.

Bree is so beautiful inside and out. She loves to be snuggled by all of us. The kids can now move freely about her, she has learned to trust. It is amazing how a little time, love and patience can teach these dogs a whole new way to love. If you could just see her right now, lying on Brysan, panting and pawing at him for some love, you'd never know she is that same dog who threatened to bite him just over two years ago. She has taught us to never give up and where there is love, there is healing.

PS: The one thing Bree loves most is the snow, I have never seen her so happy. It is such a beautiful sight watching her roll around in it literally shouting cheers of glee. Warms the heart, making it all worthwhile in the end. We feel blessed to share our lives with Bree watching her grow relax and learn to trust. Her true personality is shining through years of being in survival mode. All of these milestones helped shape the bond we now all share.

Some people may say that our pets are lucky, but we believe that we are the lucky ones to share our lives with all four of our beautiful and amazing rescued fur babies!

The Porters

Furkids: Myshia, Bree (aka Mr. Scruffles) ,Nikko & cat Denzel

Hope

In late November of 2010, I decided it was time to expand my family in the form of a furry companion. With limited knowledge and experience with dogs, I set out in the hopes of finding a relaxed, mature and special mutt. I visited the Timmins Humane Society website to get a better idea of what I could look forward to in a visit to the location. I noticed many medium sized full grown dogs that were available for adoption and got excited at the prospect of finding the perfect pooch

I visited the Humane Society with high hopes. Walking into the building that was buzzing with life, I wondered if I would find a dog that would suit my lifestyle as well as have the temperament that would allow it to live with the family cat Nelson. I introduced myself to the woman sitting at the desk and told her what I would like in a dog. She invited me to go and see the dogs they had for adoption.

I walked through the area where the dogs lived, talking about some of the dogs I had seen on the website, and others who she thought might be able to live with Nelson. Then, we walked out of this area to further discuss my possibilities. While in the main entrance way, a young looking black Lab was wandering about. She told me that this was Hope and that she was great with all of the cats and therefore was allowed to hang around at the Centre. I immediately liked Hopes' attitude toward the business of this central area.

The woman seemed to think that Hope would be a great match and I had to agree. I was advised that she was one of the easiest going dogs they had, that she did not attend to the other dogs, cats or people that came and went. It took me less than a day to decide she was the one, and returned the next day to start adoption proceedings.

I shopped for her; getting all the things I felt was necessary for a new pet. Then, I took her home with me. She was very shy, did not really respond to her name, and for the first couple of days decided to plant herself in any comfortable bed or couch. Initially, she would not come to her bowls to eat or drink, so food and water was brought to her. She was very afraid of my father, and would avoid him. Although she had some difficulty adjusting to her new home, I hoped she would become accustomed to her new environment and more confident in herself.

She is now a few years older, much more at ease with the situation she finds herself in and much more comfortable in her own fur. She has warmed up to my father and will cuddle him on the couch.

She loves to eat and has no problem getting to her bowls. She is much more playful now and understands what to do with some of her toys. She also responds to her name. She loves to walk and run with different members of the family and absolutely loves other dogs. Although she can't be trusted off leash, Hope seems to have come into her own.

In conclusion, I cannot imagine my life without Hope. She is the most wonderful dog a person could ever want. She is sweet, friendly and a great companion. I love her very much and thank everyone who had anything to do with her journey to me.

Samantha Hopson

I have never owned a dog. My parents did not approve of owning a dog while living 'in the city'. They were both raised on farms and held a belief that dogs needed the freedom to be outdoors and felt compassion for any dog locked up in a house all day. So owning a dog is something I never considered seriously. I do have some limited experience with dogs however, as both my grandparents owned dogs, on their farms, that I would play with while growing up.

When Samantha brought Hope home, I was quite reserved and was clear in my expression that this was solely her dog.........and not mine. Perhaps Hope sensed my reservation. The prevailing behavior that depicted this, is that Hope would not stay in the same room as I, if we were the only two there. This persisted for many months, despite my attempts to 'chum up'. I would walk the dog with Samantha or alone and Hope seemed fine with that, but would still vacate the room if we were alone.

Eventually Hope seemed to begin to trust me and despite initial reservation, I have come to love this dog, her gentle demeanor, her emerging playful character and extreme good looks.

Floyd Hopson

Our long and loving relationship with Moosonee Puppy Rescue (MPR) began eight years ago when I saw a friend walking one of the most beautiful and well behaved puppies I had ever seen. Guess where this pup came from? I tucked this in the back of my mind and when we moved to the country two years later, onto the MPR website I went.

There was an eight week old Rottwieller/Lab cross named Morag....love at first sight. Sadly, she was in big demand, we were fourth on the list of people wanting her. In what was meant to be, she became part of our family and is truly a spectacular dog, now six years old. We renamed her Sadie and she is our first MPR dog. I would also like to mention at this time, we met Sharron and Paul Purdy, truly angels put on earth to watch over our dear northern puppies, and I think we can now add Marilyn to that list.

Number two MPR pup came two years later, when on holiday in California, I looked on their website and there was Gus (aka Clark) looking at us with his big brown eyes. Sharron said that when people came to look at the litter, he went and sat in the corner, so no one took him, he was waiting for Sadie, Stu and I. The day we arrived home from California, Sharron and Paul came with our Gus, a Border Collie/Lab cross and the most caring and sensitive guy. We call him the Eeyore of the dog world, but at age one, he was a little too boisterous for our sedate Sadie, so I was back on the website to find Gus a playmate, preferably male, as Sadie was firmly the Alpha of our pack. I should now say that my husband has put parental controls on the MPR website to keep me out! (just kidding)

The heartbreaking Mile 26 story was there, as were two six week old red Husky crosses with beautiful blue eyes. Whistle and Steamer, male and female. Thus, came tiny Luke (aka Steamer). The most unigue, crazy dog we have ever met. Our Mile 26 puppy.

Luke arrived the same day as Barack Obama! The G-8 leaders were on their way from Huntsville to the G-20 summit in Toronto. We were on our way to the MPR in Gravenhurst, right in the middle of a massive security operation that included highway closings, choppers overhead and Luke, waiting patiently for us to bust through. He came blasting around the corner with twenty other puppies and he hasn't stopped since.

To say Luke has spirit wouldn't quite capture it. He's the most entertaining dog we've ever had. He has an entire language of his own, moaning and groaning when he has to get up in the morning, heavy sigh when he settles into his cushion, little squeaks when he wants out. He's like a Siamese cat the way he talks; sometimes he has full conversations with himself. Luke had a bit of a rough go in the beginning, chewing his way through pretty much anything that wasn't secured. Full margarine tubs, juice bottles, prescription glasses (a few of those) pens, remote controls, the keyboard off of the laptop (yup), the easy chair, plus his separation anxiety was acute. But we all persevered and he's a very settled little guy now, without losing any of his spunk.

Our pups have won the dog lottery, living in the country with lots of room to roam, and yet with owners who will drive them twenty-five minutes to go for a walk, just to give the dogs variety. Apart from the odd run-in with porcupines and skunks, country life serves them well. They now have a horse next door, something new to keep an eye on, or in Sadie's case, to guard. After the start they've had, it's an honor for us to provide our pups with a good life. They give us more than we have ever given them.

Signed: Signe & Stuart Harrison

Our story began in Orillia in October of 2010. My niece was in her second year of the Veterinary Technician Program at Georgian College. She was exposed to many dogs from various shelters but one little one caught her eye and she knew she had to find a home for her. She spoke with my husband and I at Thanksgiving and pleaded that Moonbeam was so special, and all she needed was a good home and some TLC

Up until that time, I had never heard of the Mile 26 rescue. I knew that she had to be pretty special to have survived that and for my niece to want so desperately to give her a good home. I fell in love with her from the pictures and after our first visit, knew we would be taking her home. On October 21, 2010 she came home and started her new life as 'Copper'.

To say she is a different dog today would be a gross understatement. Gone is the skittish, painfully shy dog. What's replaced it is a cautious and most times social little angel. When I first brought her home, walks were short as when we came across people and dogs, she would freeze and we would have to turn around and go home.

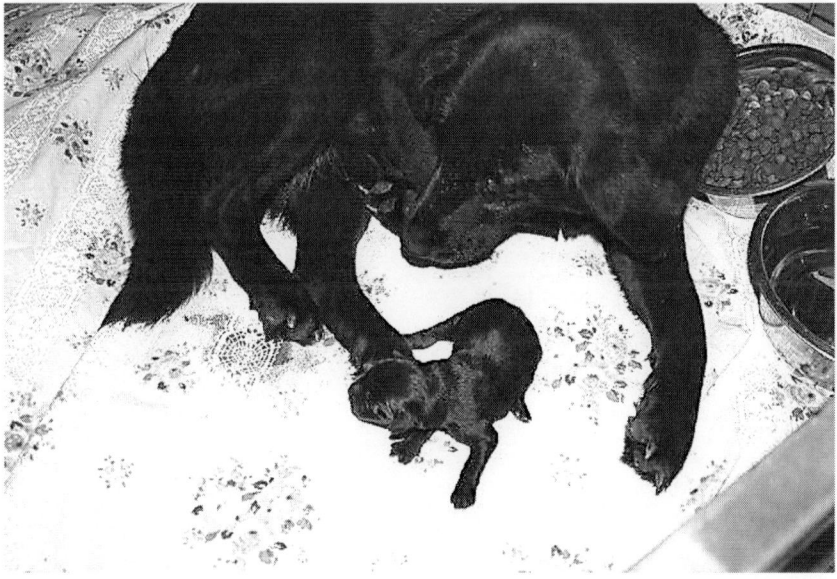

Copper (Moonbeam) in the early days at All Heart Pet Rescue with her one tiny miracle puppy named Moonshine.

Now, she pulls at the leash and whines, and can't get to dogs fast enough to say "Hi." More than one dog and she's a little more reserved, but one on one she's amazing. Surprisingly she's got a little puppy in there too that loves to come out and play. She loves to play with the puppies smaller than her, or the older dogs. The first time she played with a dog, I thought maybe they didn't like each other, so I went to pull her away. The other dog owner looked at me and said "They're playing." I didn't tell him, wow, I've never seen her play before and wasn't sure what it looked like.

She would never go to the bathroom on walks in the beginning. We would come home after walking an hour, I would then have to put her in the yard, and then she would go. Now, I've got at least four bags with me at all times. We go for walks in the trails nearby on weekends and she loves it. Just like a normal dog, she chases squirrels, not realizing she'll never be fast enough.

I've had to start monitoring how much food I give her now. For the first six months I was just happy if her bowl was half empty, now she can be a little pig! She's around fifty pounds which is ten pounds heavier than two years ago, so I have to make sure she doesn't gain any more. She's filled out quite nicely quite the carnivore. The only table scraps she's interested in is the meat. I've never seen anything like it.

She's fine around being around people. She will run up to people on our walks to smell them and if they approach slowly she will let them pet her. She has become very social and when we get together at family functions, she wants to be around all the people. She's great with us at home, and is definitely my dog as opposed to my husbands. She will sit with us when we're watching TV and has no problem around my most times, loud and busy six year old.

She normally sleeps on our bed but will also sleep with my son, whichever is warmer. She certainly likes her comfort as she doesn't spend too much time on the floor, but rather the beds and couches. She will come to me when called which is a huge step for her and seek out attention, which is another huge step.

I had no expectations when it came to Copper, never having had a rescue dog before. I can't believe the difference in two years. It took six months to realize how bushy her tail was because it was usually hidden between her legs.

She's such a loving dog. I know she will never be a carefree trusting all people kind of dog. She will always be cautious and at times very timid, and that's OK. Honestly, every month she continues to come out of her shell a tiny bit more. Someone looking in from the outside world would question my saying "She's just a different dog", but I know where she was two years ago and she is no longer in that place. Baby steps for most dogs are monumental steps for her and I'm happy if she continues to make them for the next ten or so years. She is a sweet soul, that's for sure.

Signed: Shelly

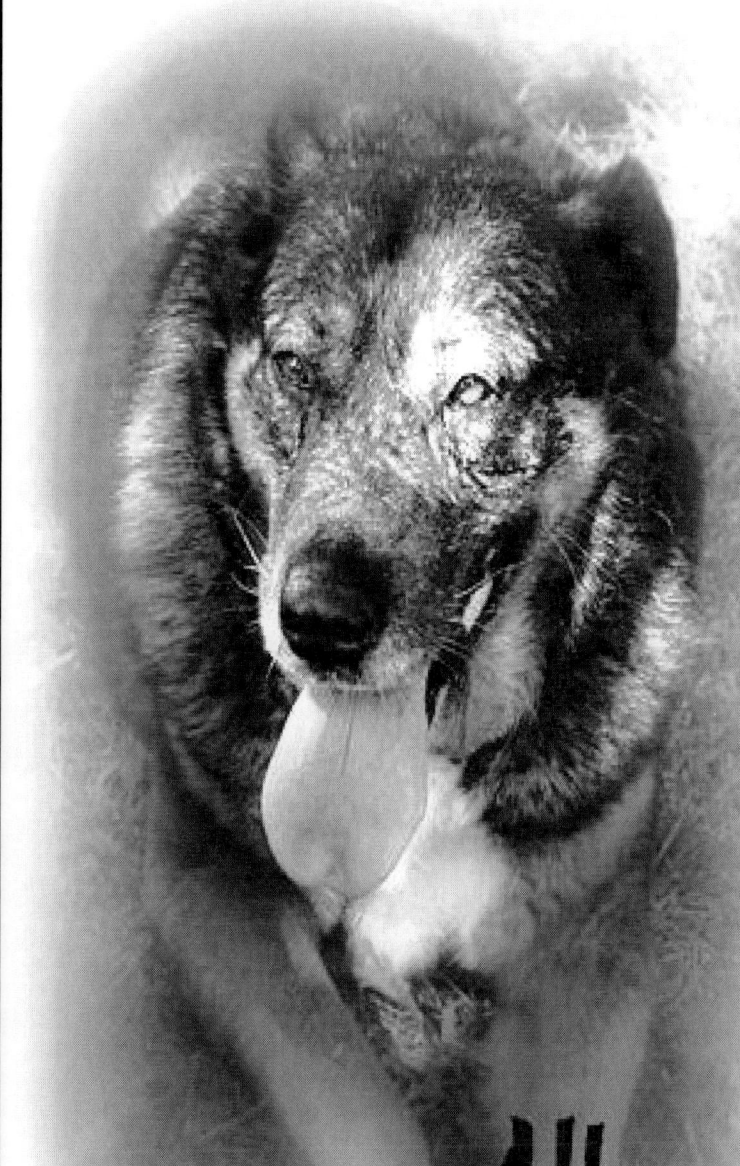

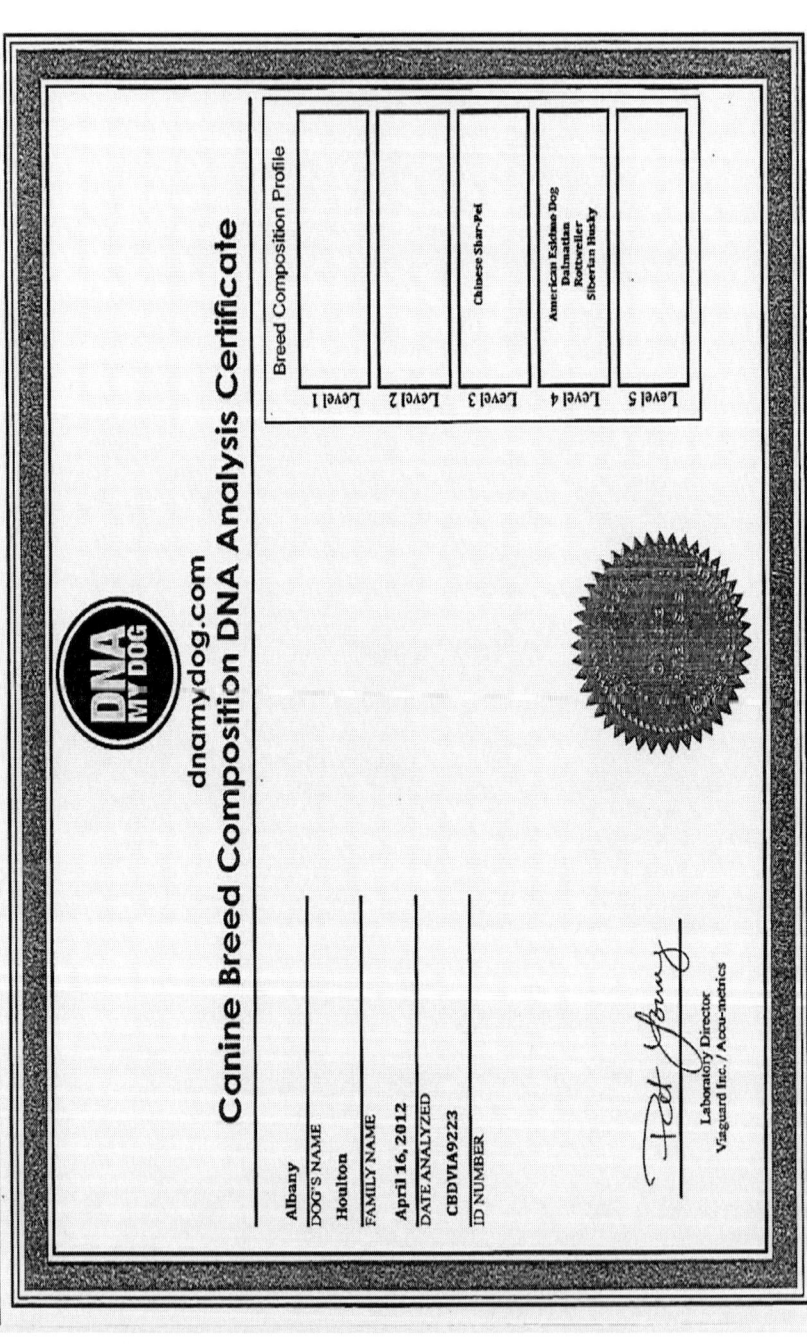

Our Mile 26 Story – Albany (Zee Zee)

As is our practice every morning, my husband and I were on the road early travelling to North Bay for work. CBC North, our usual morning listen, had just run down a quick list of the news stories for that day. I was anxiously awaiting the complete details on a group of dogs they had mentioned were abandoned in the bush north of Cochrane.

At the time we were caretakers of two wonderful Shepherd/Rottweiler mixes acquired as puppies from a couple in Bonfield about seven years ago. Neither of us had any experience with animal rescue, with the exception of a couple of turtles we had relocated when they inadvertently found their way onto our lawn. However, both of us are animal lovers and this story peaked my interest for reasons unknown to me at the time.

The news reporter finally came on the radio to explain about a man who had been caretaker for a group of stray dogs and lived with them at the Ontario Northland Rail's Mile 26 marker in the Cochrane area. The man was a hermit and his place had no road access. He had been caring for these dogs to the best of his ability. Sadly, on May 21, 2010 his cabin caught fire while cooking food for his dogs. The man perished while trying to save puppies that were inside the cabin. He left behind, approximately two-hundred dogs, with no one to take care of them. At the time of the story the OSPCA had stated that all the dogs were feral and would probably have to be destroyed. My heart went out to them and I felt helpless.

Days went by and as happens in life, work and other issues filled my mind and pushed the painful Mile 26 story to the back of my memory. Late in June, a co-worker who was considering acquiring a family pet, asked if I knew of any place to look for a dog. I decided to check on the web page of a local rescue and see what dogs they had available. There I was, scrolling through the pictures of all these beautiful babies who needed someone to love them. We had our hands full at home keeping the two dogs we had happy and healthy. Wyatt (our largest) had just recovered a couple years before from two TPLO surgeries that almost broke the bank so to speak. We had also been through the usual ailments like porcupine quills, stomach virus, etc. Still, my heart went out to all these dogs and I wanted to care for each and every one of them. I continued to scroll through the All Heart Pet Rescue page. I couldn't believe it, there they were, a group of dogs from Mile 26. How could I have forgotten about this story? Then I saw that face. The sad terrified face of a large black dog the rescue group had named Kahuna. My heart broke into a million pieces. Within seconds of seeing those pictures, I knew we had to help. We had to do whatever we could to be a part of the solution to this situation.

I gingerly introduced the idea to my husband that night on the way home. Is there a possibility that we could adopt Kahuna? Could we at least go out to All Heart and see him in person? Showing my husband the picture of this sad introverted dog sealed the deal. Next stop....All Heart Pet Rescue!

Our first trip to All Heart was in early August. All Heart has an open house every Sunday so we decided to go out and talk to the owner, Kathy Jeanneault, about possibly adopting Kahuna. We quickly learned that Kathy knows her stuff. Before even seeing Kahuna, she explained to us that he was a very disturbed dog. This group of dogs had been through a lot, and at this point Kahuna was not socialized enough to be put up for adoption. He required a lot of work before he would be ready to go into a new home. Kathy took the time to learn about our home and work situation, asked questions about what kind of time we had to offer a dog and what our property was like. She inquired about how we learned of the Mile 26 dogs and how much of the story we knew. Kathy walked us over to the dog kennel that Kahuna was staying in just to show us what she meant. The poor thing wouldn't even look at us, he coward in the corner of his kennel, head down, ears back. When Kathy walked in, he avoided her at all cost. I'm sure Kathy sensed the disappointment on my face and the heartbreak I felt for this poor animal.

She told us there was another Mile 26 dog she wanted us to meet. She said that this dog was around six years old, less active and fairly nonchalant and it's possible she would fit into our lifestyle better. That was the first time we met Albany. They brought Albany out on a leash, a feat in itself since none of these dogs were leash trained. She was shy and submissive to the point of rolling on her back as soon as I approached her. I'm not a dog expert but what I saw was a terrified dog whose' defense mechanism with humans was to be as submissive as possible. We visited for a few minutes and I informed Kathy that we would have to think about it and would be back. My heart was still broken for poor Kahuna and I wasn't sure that Albany was the dog we wanted. Luckily, I found out later, Kathy knows better.

For the next two weeks I scoured the internet to find any and all information I could about the Mile 26 dogs and their rescue. These poor souls had not only survived the fire and death of their caretaker, but had also endured bears, feral dogs and water bombers used to extinguish the bush fires that resulted from the cabin catching fire. They had spent almost a month up there by themselves. I learned that the ONR employees had submitted complaints about these dogs being left behind. The man who fed them would take the train to town and collect food. These dogs associated that train with his return. When he was alive, the train would stop at the marker so that the man could return home with what he had collected. In his passing, the train became one more danger the dogs faced every day. I also learned about the wonderful group of volunteers and ONR workers who braved bad weather, bears and other hazards to rescue as many of these animals as was possible.

After much thought, we decided to go out and visit All Heart Pet Rescue again, this time, to check in on Kahunas' progress and have another visit with Albany. I have to admit, I still wasn't one hundred percent sure about adopting her but figured the least we could do is offer her some human interaction. Upon arrival, this time, we were told that Kahunas' situation hadn't really changed much yet. Albany however was roaming free in the dog park at the rescue and we were more than welcome to go and visit with her while Kathy dealt with some other

families inquiring about adoptions.

It was a fairly warm day, and we found Albany laying in the shade of a tree 'guarded' by one of the other Mile 26 dogs. At this point in my experience with rescue dogs, I had no idea how to approach a dog properly in order to reduce the stress of the interaction on the dog. We walked up to her slowly and her reaction was to simply get up and walk away before we could even reach a hand out to pet her. She slowly rose and moved to another shady spot in the yard. We waited and after a few minutes tried to approach her again with the same results. She wasn't showing any signs of aggression toward us but she didn't want us anywhere near her.

We sat for awhile in the dog park and watched her, wondering what the heck we were doing wrong, she didn't seem this anti-social the last time we visited with her? She seemed so tired and always on the alert. All I could think about was taking her home so she could relax and get some much needed rest. Having no success, we left the dog park to go and speak with Kathy. I told her there was no way we could take this dog if she didn't want anything to do with us. I remember thinking to myself that Albany needed someone who understood more about dog socialization than we did. Kathy seemed a little disappointed but agreed that we needed to do what we felt was right. I left the rescue with a heavy heart and a promise to be back again if not to adopt, at least to visit.

On our drive home, I felt sick. I couldn't leave like this. My need to do what I could to help these poor souls was still chewing a hole through my stomach. I knew then that this wasn't over. Kathy had told us that Albany was scheduled to be spayed the first week of September. We waited until the weekend after her surgery and went to visit again.

We met Kathy in the rescue office. She was busy with other potential adopters but asked that we wait. Once she was done with the other couple she asked her daughter to bring Albany into the office. She told us about leaving Albany in the office after her surgery so she wouldn't be bothered by the other dogs. Albany had been left in the office overnight and hadn't gotten into any trouble, or messing on the floor. This answered a few questions we had since no one knew if these dogs were house trained or not. Her surgery went well but the vet had found cysts in her along with evidence that Albany had produced many litters in her time up north and her body showed it. Albany's attitude however had changed altogether.

When Maddie brought her in the room, she came running over to us and jumped up on my lap. For the next half hour or so she stayed on the couch beside us giving kisses and begging for all the attention we wanted to give her. That was all the convincing we needed. We told Kathy we would make some arrangements to take some time off work and be back to get her in a couple of days.

Two days later we arrived at the rescue to pick up the new addition to our family. We completed the necessary paperwork, received dog food and a blanket for a familiar scent for Albany and promised Kathy to return on a regular basis for visits. I'll never forget Kathy telling me how much she laughed watching us try and lift a limp, totally submissive

Albany into the back seat of our truck. Riding in a vehicle was Albany's first new experience with us and she was not overly happy about being in the truck. The drive home would take about an hour and even though I had my arm around her, she shook the whole time, I felt so bad for her. All these changes and no way of knowing that she was safe and would never have to fend for herself again.

Her new home offered a whole bunch of firsts. She didn't know how to climb stairs, a necessity to access any door in our house. Her interaction with her new pack consisted of a whole lot of lip curling and growling if our other dogs got too close or moved too fast. For the first little while she slept, but not soundly. My husband described having her as being like living with a war veteran. She would be sound asleep and then bolt upright and start growling at whichever dog was closest to her. However, through adjustment, she never once showed any aggression toward us.

Her first trip to the vet was booked right away. She was checked and her shots were brought up to date. We were told she had several dental issues and would require surgery to remove some teeth, one of which had abscessed pretty badly. We would learn later that this was a common ailment amongst the Mile 26 dogs due to the diet they were fed. We scheduled her surgery and took her home with antibiotics to reduce some of the infection. The surgery would soon be postponed.

It seems that when a female dog has a number of litters she is more susceptible to mastitis. It's a disease in which the mammary glands become infected and can flare up to the size of a baseball and if left untreated the infection can poison their whole system. Untreated the area can also become gangrenous. Over the next six months we dealt with four or five incidents of this.

The first time it happened, we were told that Albany had mammary cancer and would need all of her mammary glands removed. I didn't even want to entertain the idea of such a surgery; she had been through enough already. We gave her prescribed antibiotics and treated the infected areas as directed by our vet. The inflammation went down and we reluctantly booked the surgery. I still wasn't feeling good about this, aside the cost I had a very bad feeling in the pit of my stomach.

Three days before her surgery, we decided to take Albany for a visit to All Heart and ask Kathy for her opinion on the situation. After discussing this with Kathy and one of the volunteers at the shelter, we decided to take a leap of faith, following my intuition and cancelled the surgery. We waited, fingers crossed that I had made the right decision.

As mentioned earlier, she did have a few more incidents of mastitis, a couple of which were bad enough to cause some tissue damage and become gangrenous. I learned quickly how to detect and treat them early. She would become infected very quickly and become dehydrated with a fever. After about seven months the flare ups stopped. At one point we were told by a senior vet at our office that this would be the case due to her hormones. He also assured us that he felt there was no cancer and all would be well with time. The mastitis stopped, and Albany's tooth surgery was completed in February.

Once her health was on the right track, we started to notice huge changes in her personality. However, now she would dance for her supper, a circus act she performed by jumping up and walking on her back feet in front of you while you carried her dinner to the spot where she ate. Kathy still doesn't believe me when I tell he this, but it happens every time. The pulled back ears and slanted eyes she used to look at you with , turned up to a smile and perked up ears. The growls she would greet her brothers with became playful snaps at each other while they all run up and down the hallway to see who can get to the end first. She still is and always will be our quirky Albany and we wouldn't have it any other way.

Unfortunately, she can't be off leash in an open area. She doesn't intentionally run away but is still very controlled by her wild side. Our next venture is a huge fenced in area for her to run free. Perhaps without knowing it, she was the reason we bout a country house with one hundred acres. My only wish is that I could have helped more than one. However, all good intentions start with a dream and I have a feeling my involvement in animal rescue and rehabilitation isn't over. How could it be, I've never experienced anything else that gives you such a sense of love and satisfaction. There is nothing that can replace the look a dog gives you when she finally knows she can trust again.

Albany and her brothers Wyatt and Virgil

Albany has become so much a part of our family. I can't remember ever not having her.

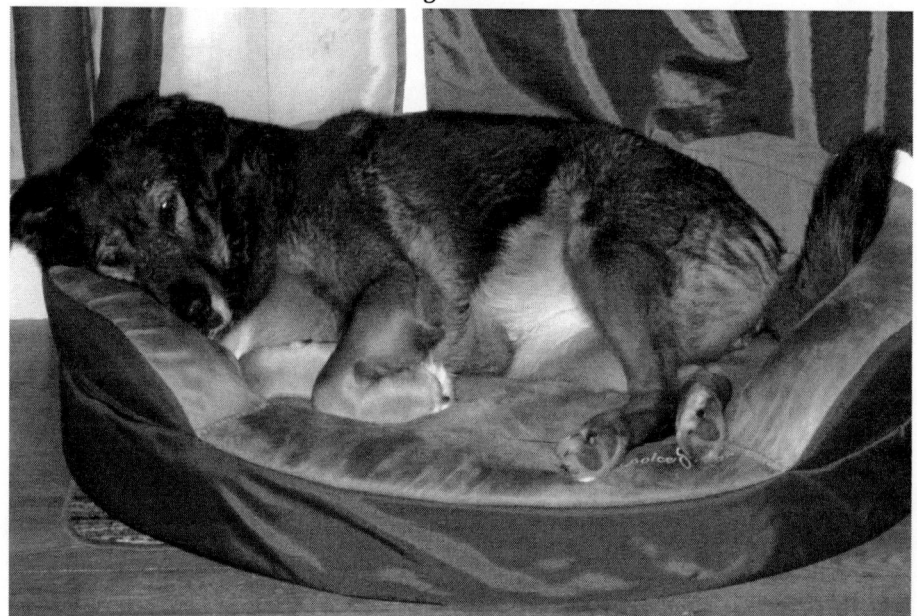

    The Mile 26 dogs are a special breed with special needs. All of the 60 plus dogs originally rescued have been re-homed with the exception of those few who passed. They have been placed with the most special group of people I have ever had the pleasure of associating with. These dogs have created a family of like minded individuals who dedicate their time and energy to a special cause. I could never express in words my gratitude to the rescuers, shelters, rehabilitators and forever homes that have created a happy ending for these animals. I fully believe our purpose in life is to make a difference in some good way. Albany has shown me how to do that. I had no idea when we adopted her that she would open up a whole new world to me. A world full of animals that need our help, any way we can and a world full of people who devote everything they have to doing just that.

    Kahuna (now Rocky) was lovingly and patiently rehabilitated by Kathy at All Heart and adopted by a wonderful couple who have dedicated themselves to his continuing success and happiness.

Lisa

http://www.youtube.com/watch?v=DXK2KZI0v48&feature=youtu.be

Please go to this link to see a beautiful song and video put together by Albany's dad Doug. He posted this around the week of the trip back to Mile 26 in July, 2011.

Oddly enough, while going through the hundreds of photos from the rescue for this book, I found one of Rocky (Kahuna) and Albany in a crate together. It appears they may have had a little history before arriving at the rescue. They travelled together on that first long journey to where they are today and I believe it was a plan all along that each of them ended up just exactly where they did.

You have to wonder where any of the Mile 26 dogs would be without Mark Zukerburg. After all, it was on Facebook that I first heard of the Mile 26 rescue. It was June 21, 2010 and thanks to a friend I was introduced to the Save The Dogs at Mile 26 page. What I discovered there was stunning. I knew right away that I had to so something to help those people. There were still so many dogs that needed saving. Thankfully I fought the desire to simply jump in my car and drive. This required some thought and planning, of course, this was a job for OERS. As a member of a Disaster Response Team dedicated solely to animal rescue, I figured this would be a perfect deployment for us. I quickly emailed our director of Operations, Mike Belanger, and explained the situation to him.

I cannot even describe my shock when I read his return email and learned that he did not share my opinion. This was not something OERS would get involved in. He raised some very valid points, but I persisted. Within a day he had changed his mind. OERS was going to Mile 26. As I waited anxiously for the details to be worked out, I followed the events closely on Facebook. From there, I was able to get a real understanding of the conditions we'd be going into. I was both physically and mentally prepared, I just had to wait for the word of our pending departure. That word never came. As our plans were coming together, public pressure was pushing the OSPCA to come up with their own plans. Suddenly they were ready to respond. They were going in, we were not.

While I fully understood the complexities of the situation and reluctantly accepted the facts that OERS would not be deploying, I could not simply walk away. I had to do something. When I explained this to Mike, he was kind enough to pass on the contact information of the lady he'd been working with. Maybe she had a job for me.

When I first spoke with Sharron Purdy she explained that the real crisis at that point was not getting the dogs out, but rather getting them moved. Rescue and foster homes in Northern Ontario were beyond capacity. She needed somewhere for them to go. I quickly offered to get the word out and find as many foster or adoptive homes as I could. Sharron already had several Mile 26 dogs in her care and if she could get them placed, she could bring down more.

Several days later, I found myself pulling into the parking lot at Cookstown Outlet Mall where I was supposed to meet up with Sharron's' husband Paul and pick up two dogs I had arranged fostering for. One named Cosmos was going to be fostered by a friend's coworker. This lady and her daughter sounded perfect for the frightened, submissive dog Sharron had described. Carla, the other one, was coming home with me.

When I first offered my help to Sharron and explained my background, Carla's name came up almost immediately. Sharron explained that Carla was not like the other dogs. While the majority of these dogs were dealing with the new fear and stress in their lives with a flight response, Carla preferred to fight. Sharron could tell that somewhere inside there was a perfectly nice dog just waiting to get out, but there were some mighty big barriers standing in her way. Carla would be very difficult to place, but with my background and the amazing Jim Tsitanidis, K9 Trainer and Behavioral Consultant committed to helping me, I might be Carla's only hope. If I really wanted to help, it was Carla who most needed me.

I have to admit, I was really kind of hoping to take on one of those scared souls who I knew I could bring out of their shell with some simple old fashioned TLC. A cranky old girl was not at all what I had hoped for, but the offer had been made and if this was were I could be most effective, well how bad could it be?

My first three minutes with Carla should have indicated what I was getting into. Thankfully I was either not perceptive enough or just too pig headed to fully comprehend the magnitude of what I was taking on. When I pulled up to Paul's truck, he was standing outside with a beautiful albeit terrified black lab type dog with the most incredible blue eyes. This was Cosmos. I slowly greeted her and got her settled in my car. Now it was time to meet the other one. Carla. Paul explained that she would be best transported in the kennel she was in because, well, there was no other option. As he opened the door, I understood. Inside was a snarling, large, short mass of black with angry eyes and bared teeth. This was not the hero's welcome I had hoped for from my new charge, but it was early, she just needed to get used to me.

Carla's first night at our home was both fright filled and horrifying ...for me! The stress of the day had taken its' toll on the poor girl and on the way home, the contents of her once filled belly had made its' way out from every available orifice. The dog and the kennel were a mess, so our first stop was on the back deck. Once I was sure the gate was secure and my other dogs were confined inside, I opened the crate to lt her out. She growled. For half an hour I tried my best to coax her out. She growled some more. Finally, I gave up and went in the house. Another half hour passed but finally she decided to venture out of her crate. As I came out the back door, to congratulate her, she scooted into the corner behind the BBQ and growled. Not wanting to stress her any more, I quickly set to work at getting the kennel cleaned and set up for her in the house. I concluded that Carla herself would not be getting cleaned up any time soon, but much of the goo was being left all over the deck so how bad could that be?

   Since I knew there was no way Carla could escape the backyard, I left her out there to settle. That was fine until evening set in and I realized I would somehow need to get this dog inside the house and into her kennel. She was now letting me pet her, so I figured slipping a collar and leash onto her would not be a problem. I was wrong, very wrong! Suddenly though', I understood completely why Paul had handed me a slip lead before he drove off. It was time to lasso my new little friend. We had to get into the house and off to bed. The plan sort of worked. After only a few minutes I managed to get the lead over her head and get her close to the door. Then she decided she was done and went into what I refer to as a 'death roll' slipping out of the lead, running back behind the BBQ. On the third attempt, I had her inside, right in front of the kennel door. That's when she made her final slip, but at least she was in the house, we just needed to get her into the kennel.

   Of course this change in surroundings combined with five extra people who had come to check out the new dog, pushed Carla over the edge. She defaulted into a fight mode and snapped at any well meaning kid who thought that they could whisper her into that kennel. Feeling frustrated, I took a few minutes to regroup and watch these dumb kids fail. However, when their efforts ha driven the divine Miss. C and her angry claws onto my antique table; where she held court barking and snapping at anything that moved, it was time to shut my helpers down. I sent them all away and started to explain to this new household member that her behavior was not appropriate. Nobody was going to hurt her and we just wanted to get along. She growled. In utter frustration I walked away, Carla hopped down and ran into her kennel.

   At this point I would have been quite happy to call a close to Day One and go to bed, and almost did, but then a feeling of horror struck. I had booked a vet appointment for Carla for the next morning. How could I possibly get her there when I couldn't even get a collar on her? In all my time doing Animal Control, I had never once been unable to walk into that clinic with a dog on a lead. I had to call Jim.

Jim arrived at nine the next morning. We had an hour and a half to tame the beast and get her to her appointment. No easy task, but this was Jim. I watched and studied as he worked his magic. She bit her way out of two slip leads, put up quite a fight, but eventually submitted to Jim. At ten thirty, Jim and I walked Carla into the vet clinic where she was an absolutely perfect patient. From palpitation to vaccinations to nail clipping, she took it all in stride without so much as a curled lip, though it would have had to curl through the muzzle!

Before Jim left, he helped me put together a rehab plan for Carla. Along with the list of homework, he invited us to be part of his next obedience class in a week's time. I had always liked and admired Jim, but on that day he officially reached hero status. With his help, we were going to turn this dog around and make her highly adoptable. How hard could it be?

Over the next few weeks Carla's life changed drastically. She quickly realized that she was running with a new pack and there was a new alpha bitch to deal with. No longer could she march to the beat of her own drum. Oddly, she couldn't have handled the change any better. As more and more structure took over her life, she responded with newfound calmness and confidence. As long as she had me to hide behind, there was nothing too big or scary to take on except thunder, fireworks and gunshots. Those were still terrifying. Although she was not a fan of any obedience nonsense, she did learn to love praise. The first time I saw Carla bouncing up and down with pride, I cried. My

frightened, angry foster was finally filled with happiness. By mid October, just three months after her arrival, the transformation was complete. Carla had graduated Obedience School and learned to live in a household with other dogs, kids and a little rabbit that she absolutely adored. I had done what I set out to do. Excitedly I emailed Sharron to let her know that Miss. Carla was ready for adoption.

Sharron reminded me that even the new and improved Carla would not be the easiest dog to place. There aren't a whole lot of people in the market for a vertically challenged older dog with issues. I told her I was in no hurry. Carla was welcome to stay for as long as it took. The important thing was, to find the right family that would continue to provide the structure Carla needed in order to continue to thrive. Besides, now that she wasn't trying to rip us apart, the old cranky girl was kind of growing on me.

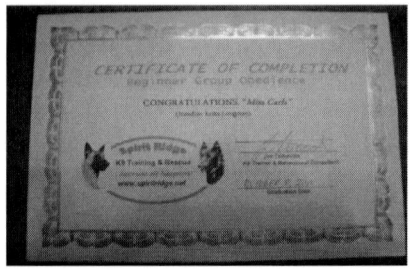

Several months passed and although a few people expressed interest in Carla, they quickly backed away due to her background. Then in late January, Sharron contacted me saying there was a really good prospective home and they wanted a meeting. On a cold and crisp Saturday, Carla and I hopped in the car to make the long drive to meet these people. The entire way there, I wrestled with mixed emotions. I really wanted this to work out, fostering is a temporary situation and the job is not finished until the animal is placed in a new home. I had so much time and energy invested in Carla and she had come such a long way that I couldn't settle for half measures now. Only the perfect home would do.

By the time we arrived I was ready to find any fault I could with these people. I couldn't. What I found was a perfectly lovely retired couple who absolutely adored their pets. They were kind and loving. We had a nice visit and they seemed to like Carla even though she wasn't quite the outgoing girl they expected. On the way home, I was feeling even more conflicted. As great as these people were, I still had a nagging feeling that this wasn't right. Was I being over critical? Was I just looking for an excuse to keep this old cranky girl because giving her up would be difficult?

At home I sat down to send Sharron a recap of our visit. As I typed about how nice these folks were, it suddenly occurred to me, maybe that was the problem. They were too nice. Carla would be loved, no doubt, but would she get the structure and discipline that had allowed her to overcome her fears? Sharron completely understood my reservations and agreed that we should take a few days to weigh this out. Carla's options were limited, could this work? How bad could an abundance of love be?

Sometimes fate is a wonderful thing. While Sharron and I struggled to make the right decision for Carla, those wonderfully loving people proved that they were also incredibly insightful. They too had been thinking a lot and decided they were not the right home for Carla.

Although I was happy with the decision, I was completely exhausted from the events of the previous week. I didn't know how many times I could go through that process. But then again, this was Carla we were talking about. How long would it be before anyone expressed an interest? I knew Sharron was putting a lot of time and energy into trying to find Carla a home and I knew that energy would be better spent on the endless stream of puppies that were once again coming her way. Although it meant that I would once again fail at fostering, I decided that the best decision for all concerned would be for me to keep Carla.

On February 1, 2011 we officially became a three dog household again. The cranky old girl was staying right here. Now there are two of us!

Erika Longman

Carla today, happy in her new pack and forever home.

Dakota

Dakota, where to start? Amanda, my wife, wanted a puppy. I suggested we adopt and took a trip out to All Heart Pet Rescue to look at some dogs with our kids. We were looking at all the dogs running around and one stood out. 'Dakota'

He was shy and a little bit skittish but such a good boy. He wasn't adopted because he couldn't be let off his leash. Now he plays and runs around the yard with no fence and even lets himself out through the screen door if he needs to take care of business.

I have seen where and what he came from and he is a lucky boy. Thanks to everyone who helped him on his journey of life.

Clayton, Amanda, Nick, Aryn and Alex

The magnificent Dakota. He is now a happy and confident boy with his very own forever family.

Dakota and the Mile 26 gang at All Heart Pet Rescue.

Look at those tails!

We adopted Ruby on August 16, 2010 from the Clarington Animal Shelter. She was born on Canada Day and is one of the pups from the girls who came to the shelter from Mile 26.

When Ruby was just a baby, we took her on her first adventure in life. We decided to go camping up in Hunstsville for the week. Being a

chubby, furry little puppy, she wasn't very excited and slept a lot, unless a chipmunk ran through our camp site. One day while camping, we came back to our site and saw several people running up the road toward us yelling that there was a bear in the park. Just as we went to grab Ruby to put her in our truck, a big bear wandered into our site. Ruby put her back hair up and started to charge at the bear. At the time, it was very scary trying to get her away from the bear, but now we look back on it and see this little puppy, barking her head off at this huge animal many times her size.. We knew that she would grow up protecting us.

Speaking of growing up, she certainly tested our patience along the way. We had just purchased our first home and bought ourselves new furniture and were starting to build some pride in our new purchases. Being our first puppy, we had a lot to learn. New furniture would become chew toys and carpets became pee pads. Paper towel and floor cleaner became regular purchases, of that we were not so proud, but she had a certain way of gaining our love. As she grew, my husband would take her everywhere in the truck and she loves her little trips to the hardware store or the garbage dump. She's definitely Daddy's truck dog.

One specific day last summer, we took her down to the beach. She was in the back seat, bouncing around very anxiously watching the birds and people, everything that moved. All of a sudden, she leaped out of the window and ran across the beach. I ran after her and there she was, lying between a couple who had been sleeping on the beach. Talk about embarrassing......waking someone up in order to pry your dog out from between them.

On January 4, 2011 Ruby, now about six months old, was preparing for her first night at the end of our bed. She had proven to us she wouldn't chew us out of bed and home. As she started to settle and calm down for the evening, she started to whine and whimper. Being the first night, we didn't give it much notice and told her to be quiet. Now, as my husband and I were starting to fall into a deeper sleep, Ruby began to get very restless and started bouncing around the bed and attempts to quiet this young pup were failing. I thought to myself that this would be the first and last night she would be in our bed. At roughly two a.m. our tame little dog went off the handle, barking frantically at our bedroom window. I drew back the curtains to reveal thirty foot high flames coming off of the house next door. The flames were getting so close, that our siding had started to melt. To make a long story short, our new little puppy had managed to wake us in desperation, saving us, our three cats and our home. A very quick response by the Port Hope Fire Department was able to save our house from despair. To this day, our little Ruby has earned her place at the foot of our bed, in our home and definitely in our hearts

It is easy to say that this dog has made us laugh, scared us, angered us, embarrassed us, but most of all made us love her. She has been a part of our family now for over two years and I wouldn't trade her for the world.

Thank you for your interest in our little fur ball. It has been an honor and a joy to have the opportunity of sharing our story with you.

Daniel and Amy Janes

In April of 2010 I started on a hunt for a puppy, but it was very important to my family that we rescue a dog and not buy from a breeder. I searched the internet and different websites and just happened to come across the Moosonee website and started reading the stories about the dogs. Then I clicked on to the Mile 26 information and read all about the incredible rescue of all the puppies and I knew then I had to have one of these babies.

I spoke with Sharron, I believe her name was and inquired about the dogs she had. She informed me that she had five puppies that were a lab/collie cross. In June 2010, we arranged a day where her husband drove all the way from the Moosonee Puppy Rescue in Bracebridge to my home in Scarborough. When her husband arrived, there were five cute little faces running around my back yard. My husband and two children were there and we were all playing with the puppies. I remember asking what names they were given and was told of all the cute rail yard names. After playing with the puppies for awhile, I wanted all of them but could only take one.

We had noticed Switch right away. He was all black like the other puppies, but the only one with white under his neck and paws and right under his chin.

My husband and I said, "That's our puppy, we want him." So that day we filled out all the paperwork and Switch has been our baby boy ever since. We decided to keep his name the same, for us it's the reminder of what he went through and where he came from. We love Switch with all of our hearts and soul, he is another child for us.

When we got Switch, he weighed about ten pounds or so, now two years later he weighs eighty-seven pounds and is a very big dog. He is very protective of us all especially when a stranger comes around. I remember one time when we took him to the dog park. My husband and Switch went right in to the far end of the park and I stayed close to the fence. When I walked in, a dog came rushing at me barking and from the other end of the park, Switch ran to me and scared the dog away. He melts my heart with his eyes, he is the most beautiful dog.

We had a scare with our boy last year. We were at my sons' hockey game and came home to Switch as normal, only this day, I realized that he had gotten hold of my asthma inhaler. He seemed fine at first but then a few hours later he was very lethargic and wasn't himself. I am the one who takes Switch for his last walk in the evening, he wouldn't get up and we had to rush him to the Birchmount Animal Hospital at eleven-thirty pm. He was poisoned by the inhaler, close to death and we got him there just in time. He spent ten hours in intensive care and we called every hour to check on our baby. None of us could sleep or eat, we were so worried. With God's blessing no doubt, our boy made it through and we picked him up eighteen hours later, one of the most intense but happiest moments of our lives. The bill was a hefty one but he is another child for us and we couldn't imagine our lives without him.

Thank you for telling the stories of these amazing dogs that were rescued.

Shirley Lake & Family

Kodiak

Who knew that a visit to my local small town cheese shop in the fall of 2010 would result in getting our 'furever' little friend? A discussion with the cheese clerk about Moosonee Puppy Rescue, lead me to a visit of their website. By visiting the website, we learned of the Mile 26 rescue and the dogs. Reading more about the courageous rescue, we learned that one dog in particular named Stillwater, had a litter of puppies and were available with Moosonee. It was at that moment that directly in front of us was the first ever picture of our future family member, Kodiak (aka Grove), and there began our adventure.

I don't know if all northern dogs come with the same type of personality, but ours has quite a unique one. We were told she was part Husky and Shepherd that is the furthest from the truth. She is Husky, Chow, Cocker Spaniel, Labrador and Rhodesian Ridgeback. That's quite a lot for one dog, but we wouldn't have it any other way.

She has all the independence of a Husky, the beautiful coloring of a red Chow all the way to the longer hair of a Cocker Spaniel. Let's not forget the ridge on her back that stands up like a Mohawk when she gets scared. But one of her best traits comes from the Labrador. We have a pool in our backyard. Kodiak loves the water so much that she will sit on the top step of the deck and whimper that she wants to go in for her daily swim. We will let her go and she can fly through the air and clear half the pool before hitting the water.

Kodiak also loves to talk to you, chase her tail and play tag. Sometimes I look at her and she has such a sad look in her eye that must tell the story of all of those courageous dogs that have survived such an ordeal. My family gives thanks every day for what all the rescue organizations did and all of those souls who both survived and didn't. You made it possible for us to get our FUREVER friend Kodiak. Our lives are so much more complete with her in it.

The Michalowicz Family

Woody

After the passing of our two senior cats Jessie and Jake, we began the search for a long promised puppy (or two). We were determined to find a shelter puppy, but found that difficult to do in Toronto. Shelters rarely have puppies for long, demand outnumbering supply. We did find and adopt two shelter kittens as we looked, making the search for a puppy (or two) more urgent. We had hopes of raising the kittens Dakota and K.C. with a puppy.

We stumbled onto Petfinder.com and by entering our desired breed of Labrador Retriever, we eventually heard the saddest story of a man perishing in a fire in Northern Ontario, leaving hundreds of dogs to be taken care of. One particular story caught our heart, a pup that had hidden in a woodpile for three days and nights after the disaster. A little black pup was rescued by Ontario Northern Railway workers who had heard the pup from inside the stack of wood but weren't able to reach him until day three.

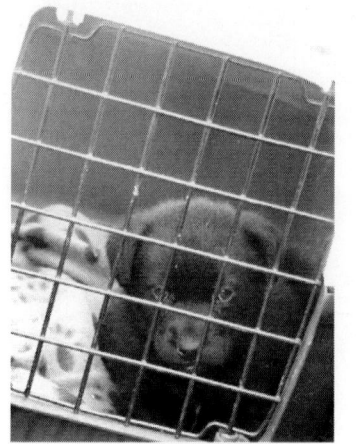

The pup was reunited with his littermates by Heidi Pratt, except Josie, who had also hidden under rotting floor boards in an old shack during all of the commotion. In Bracebridge at Moosonee Puppy Rescue, a pup fittingly named Woody was posted as available for adoption on their website. We quickly applied and got to meet Woody and some of his litter siblings right in our own backyard a few days later. From Mile 26 to Bracebridge to Toronto. What a trip!

That was June 27, 2010 and Woody is now more than two years old. He has become an excellent role model to our newest canine addition Foley, a three legged pup from Moosonee. Woody is a sensitive, fun loving dog. He doesn't like may other small dogs except his girl friend Roxy and Foley of course.

Woody like sticks, balls, bones and long walks. His favorite place to sleep is on the couch, which he prefers not to share. Woody is stubborn, easily spooked and howls at fire trucks. He enjoys the sounds of trains and small planes. He will forever be a Northern Ontario Dog, even though he now lives in the city.

Sweetness and Joy to Woody!
Michael & Laura Franklin

Woody is a true survivor of the Mile 26 Rescue. To survive the time he did, terrified and hiding under a woodpile with no food or water at such a tender young age is a miracle. The fact that he was even discovered in

all the rubble and confusion sure says he is meant to be here and for a very special reason. He'll always be remembered by the Mile 26 family as the little puppy in the woodpile.

I got Flynn in August of 2010 from Clarington Animal Shelter. I had lost my dog 'Q' in May after a year filled with tragedy. I was very depressed and Lacey my twelve year old Aussie/Border Collie was also depressed and I thought a puppy would help her. I didn't feel ready for a puppy, thinking that I was too sad and would be bad for a puppy.

My friend Michelle was at the Clarington Animal Shelter dropping off dog licenses and they had a litter of puppies that had been born two weeks earlier. She went in to see them and there was one tan color boy in a litter of black puppies. 'Q' was a reddish brown Shepherd/Malamute cross. So she sent me a picture of him. Michelle said I should go and see them and told me the Mile 26 story. I did go and see them when they were five weeks old. I sat with the puppies and their mother Nellie. She was fine with me being there and she lay down away from her kids and relaxed.

Mile 26 Nellie's babies born at Clarington Animal Shelter

At that visit, there was also another litter that had been born from Mile 26 (Sophia/Klute) I visited both litters and took some pictures. I looked up the Mile 26 rescue on the internet and looked at all of those pictures thinking how the pound puppies might grow up. I still didn't think I should get a puppy but looking at pictures on the internet was kind of comforting. I checked Kijiji and Petfinders and saw a posting for the puppies at the Clarington Shelter with a picture of the brown puppy from the July 1st litter, when he was eight weeks old. I decided that I would go to the shelter before work on Saturday to see if he was still there, because it seemed like a message that it was that brown puppy in the internet posting.

When I got there, still undecided about what I should do, I found that there were three puppies from that litter left, one was the brown puppy. I went to the dog runs to see them and said I was surprised to see them still there. The shelter attendant said that two people had already tried to adopt him but were not approved, so I assumed this meant that I was supposed to adopt him. I had to go to work and the shelter wanted to microchip, give him his shots and bath him, so I would have to come back later to get him.

So I went to work, bathed the dogs I was grooming then went back to the shelter to get my new son who had his bath at the shelter. The first thing a groomer wants to do with a new pet is give it a bath but I had to wait a couple of days because of the microchip. While I was picking him up, his two remaining brothers were being adopted together.

My puppy became Flynn a few days later, after researching names and finding that Flynn means red in Gaelic. He does make Lacey very happy, she loves to have a boy to boss around and he has learned that when playing with her, he's not allowed to touch her, she's very strict. He also fit in very well with my beagle Buddy; they have become best friends but can get up to no good together.

Flynn was a perfect puppy, very easy to housetrain and good with other dogs. He has grown to be a medium sized boy who is loving and affectionate with people he has known since he was a puppy. Flynn has

taken puppy class basic manners, some Rally O classes and he has a novice trick dog title. He does have some fear issues that we are working on. I am glad that I adopted him and he does make me happy even if he is a lot of work.

Patricia Nolan

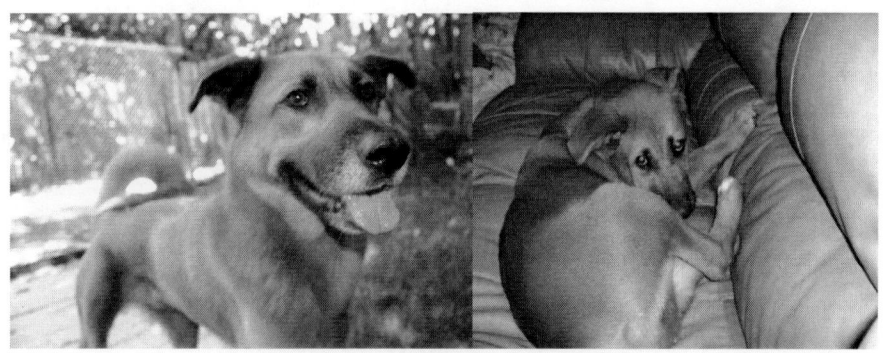

Sophia

We first heard about the Mile 26 rescue from my mom, who had temporarily fostered three black female dogs. After hearing about it, I looked into this wonderful thing that people had done in rescuing all of these dogs. I then got in touch with someone from one of the rescues involved and told her that I had lost my best friend almost a year and a half ago, and although I had not wanted to get another dog because of how much her passing had devastated me, I wanted to help one of these wonderful dogs.

At that time, I was told there were only two dogs left that were not already adopted or fostered and they were being kept in a shelter. Greg and I drove out to meet Sophia (aka Clute) and Nellie on a Saturday in early September 2010 at Clarington Animal Shelter. We were told that one of the girls was still nursing her litter and the other one had a litter as well, but they were all adopted now, and she was becoming very withdrawn and depressed. When we first walked in to the shelter, Sophia was behind the counter with the girls. When they brought her out, I saw how low her nipples hung and had to fight back my tears. They put a lead on her and let me walk her. As soon as we got outside, I bent down, hugged her and cried into her coat. Just to think of the life she must have lived up to that point broke my heart.

About a half hour later, we went back inside to go and meet Nellie. We were told she was very timid and nervous at first, but once she gets to know & trust you, she will become a 'lap dog'. The girl walked around the corner with her and as soon as she saw us, strangers, she stopped dead in her tracks, tail went down between her legs and she pulled to go back to the safety of her cage.

Greg and I followed her and the girl outside into the run where we sat on the ground in the middle of the run so we wouldn't seem so big and scary to her. Nellie was on the left side of us, but her run was on the right so she had to get past us to get to her run which was closed. She immediately started pawing frantically at Sophia's cage door to try and get in with her, when she realized she couldn't, she ran past us like a bullet. Because her cage door was closed too, her legs started to shake, her tail between her legs, so frightened she peed, laid down and pressed herself against her cage door. We did not push her and because Sophia was still nursing and we were advised to return the next week.

That entire week, all I could think about was bringing those two precious girls home. The following Saturday, we made our way back to pick up 'our girls'. Nellie had to be lifted into the car because she was so scared, and they both laid flat on the floor in the back seat for the entire ride home. I don't think they had ever seen a car before except for being transported from Mile 26. When we got home, Sophia immediately rolled around in our backyard, seemingly feeling right at home but Nellie was very unsure and nervous. I had to carry her into the house because she couldn't get in on her own.

As the first few months went by, I noticed that they never barked and their tails were always down. Any loud bang while we were walking outside and they would both jump out of their skins and try to run home. They just didn't seem happy; it was like their spirits were broken. The only thing we could do was give them as much love as they could handle and time. That was fine with us, they could have all the time they needed.

As time went by, the other neighbors with dogs noticed that slowly they seemed to look a little more at ease when they were out walking. Nellie didn't try to run the other way every time she saw a person in the distance. After many months, she started to pull only to cross the street as the person got near us. Sophia for the first many months would walk either beside us or slightly behind with her head and tail always down.

After about nine months, slowly but surely, bit by bit, each of them started to blossom in their own unique ways. I noticed Sophia was actually getting a spring in her step; she no longer walked behind us with her head and tail down. Nellie would actually get excited when she heard the word walk, and the rattling of the leashes. Slowly their tails started to raise, first at half mast and now after more than two years, both tails are raised fully when they are out for walks. They have a bounce in their walk and both finally get excited when we come home, they actually come to greet us at the door. Nellie gets so excited when we get her leash, she runs and grabs a toy then leaps onto their couch and starts to sing (howl). It's the cutest thing I've ever seen.

The newest thing with Sophia is every night after dinner, she gets frisky and playful. She'll sit on her couch and start whining. After a few minutes one of our older cats, Andy, hears her and comes peeking around the corner. Sophia jumps down and they both do a dance, Sophia nudges Andy's body with her head then jumps back. She'll keep doing this until he swipes at her with his paw, then start all over again. Any has taken a real liking to her, and most nights they sleep side by side.

Nellie is a little love bug who follows me everywhere. She loves to sleep beside me on the bed, though it gets cramped sometimes. Sophia on occasion feels left out and joins us for cuddles and snuggles. It has been amazing to watch how much they have both changed, from nervous Nellie and withdrawn Sophia to the happy, relaxed and playful girls they have become.

It has now been over two years that we've had these precious girls. They both still don't bark, but that will come too. Only once when Greg was walking Sophia late at night and she barked when she noticed someone out in their yard. She actually growled and we thing she was protecting Greg.

They have both come such a long way, learning to trust and finally seem to feel joy. Now they can just be 'dogs' and enjoy things that dogs enjoy. Watching them develop and bloom was, and continues to be, one of the most rewarding things we have ever experienced. Both Greg and I are looking forward to many more years of happiness with them. We love them more than life itself.

Catherine Fuessel and Greg Best

Nellie
August, 2010

Nellie's Puppies.

Sophia's first meeting at Clarington Shelter. Oh that face!

Our girls!

Our Story of Meeting Gardiner, a Survivor of Mile 26

On March 17, 2010 I suffered a near fatal pulmonary embolism and spent a week in hospital. When I was discharged, I could not walk to the end of my driveway and back. The doctors told me that could be all the mobility I may have. Over time, I could walk a little more each week, but it was hard to stay motivated.

We back onto a green belt and one day in May, a cream colored tomcat decided to spend the weekend on our back deck. We did not feed him but he would not move on. My wife who has three rescued cats already, made the decision after three days, to take him to Clarington Animal Shelter, they did not have a lot of cats at the time, so they took him in. We agreed that if he was not adopted out after four or five weeks, that we would take him in as a house cat.

Six weeks went by and he was still there, so on Friday we went to visit him. At this time, Clarington was bursting with thirty kittens; there was no way an adult male was going to be adopted any time soon, so we took him in. While I was there I decided to take a peek in at the dogs. My wife gave me 'stink eye' as I walked in to the kennel. The dogs started barking for attention and jumping up and down, except for one tan dog that just lifted his head from his cot, looked over at me and laid his head back down.

He just seemed so indifferent to his surroundings and sad. I asked to take him to the outside enclosure. There is a bench that my wife and I sat down on and let him off his lead and all he wanted to do was sit next to my wife. He seemed content to be near us and wasn't interested in running around like you would expect from a dog who had been cooped up inside. By this time, I was walking farther each day and thought this dog and I might be a good fit for each other. So we went in and talked with the staff and asked if we could adopt him, but with the provision that the cats came first and if it didn't work out, they would take him back.

That is when we first heard the story of Mile 26 and learned his name, Gardiner. Because of the special nature of Gardiner's situation, they agreed to our request. The next day we took him home. He had no interest in the cats, or they with him.

   I had my walking partner! Gardiner has been my motivation. On the days I am low and do not want to go out, I look at him and think of what he has gone through and I do not want to let him down, so we go.

   My wife and he have become such friends. She looks after him and in truth, now that I am back at work, takes him for his week day walks. My brother in law and Gardiner have also become great friends and he will take him out for his after dinner walks during the week too.

   On behalf of my family, we wish to thank you all for your efforts in saving this dog, who has saved me.

Paul and Julie Heldsinger, and Stephen Kinnear

This was Gardiner shortly after his rescue at Mile 26. Wet, tired, frightened and hungry. But now on his way to a better life.

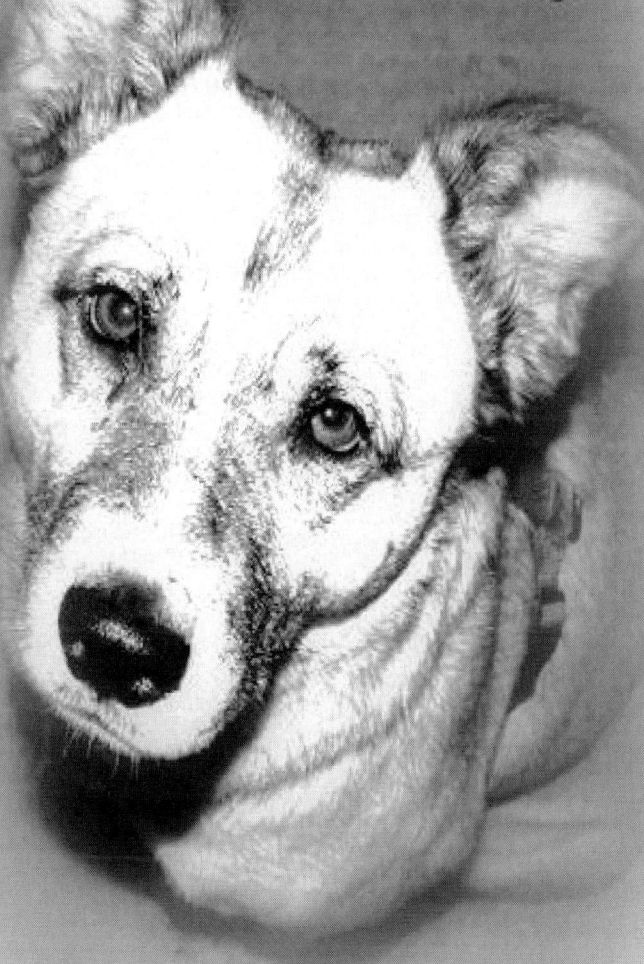

We are a family of four. Beckie (mommy), Bob (daddy), Delanie aged 11 and Gracie aged 8. We already had a dog, a Border Collie named Shiloh, but the girls wanted a puppy. We searched the rescues online, came across Petsave and fell in love with Frankie and Schizzle.

We called and set up an appointment to meet little Frankie. When we got there, Jill told me the story of Mile 26, which I did know about but didn't know Frankie was a Mile 26 dog. She told me Frankie had been adopted, but after seven months was returned because he chewed drywall. The owners tried crating him but it only made his behavior worse. Anyway, we met Frankie and he was shy and unsure, but I didn't care, this little guy would eventually come home with us, I knew it in my heart.

The second time I went to see him; he was outside and ran right to the fence with his tail wagging. I knew then and there that I had to give this baby a chance so for two weeks we visited and walked him. Reluctantly, Jill brought him to spend a night with us to see how Shiloh would react. Shiloh was aggressive for a day, and then they became buddies. By the way, that night lasted forever, because he never returned to Petsave.

He missed his shelter companion Schizzle, so my youngest daughter bought him a stuffed dog that resembled her. The first three months,

Frankie chewed everything while we were out. He ran away twelve times in the first four months, but the last four times he came home all on his own. An open door is no longer scary, as he goes out and stays in the yard. He has learned to sit, stay and shake a paw, and has adjusted to a crate which he sleeps in and is never locked unless a necessity. He loves swimming, running along beside a bike and his walks. Frankie loves kittens and some cats, absolutely loves every dog he meets.

Frankie has been known to take food outside to feed stray kittens. We discovered this after wondering why he was taking his food outdoors to eat. A little stray had been hiding in our yard and Frankie was feeding it. He also saved one from a pile of rubble while on one of our walks not too long ago. He wouldn't leave the site and rummaged and dug until he found her. We foster many kittens and grown cats. Frankie seems to want to share with them, maybe remembering the days he needed help.

Frankie is a part of our family and we would be lost without him. Can't say enough, but I love the beautiful little dog he has turned into. He is loved by everyone who meets him.

Bob, Beckie, Delanie and Gracie

Delanie asked for donations of food, toys and other supplies for the animals at the shelter, in lieu of gifts for her Birthday party. I see a future animal rescue lady here, with generosity like this!

Frankie's pack mate Shiloh.

Frankie visits Santa!

A poem written by a very special young lady. You are the future hope for our companion animals in need and I'm so proud to know you Delanie.

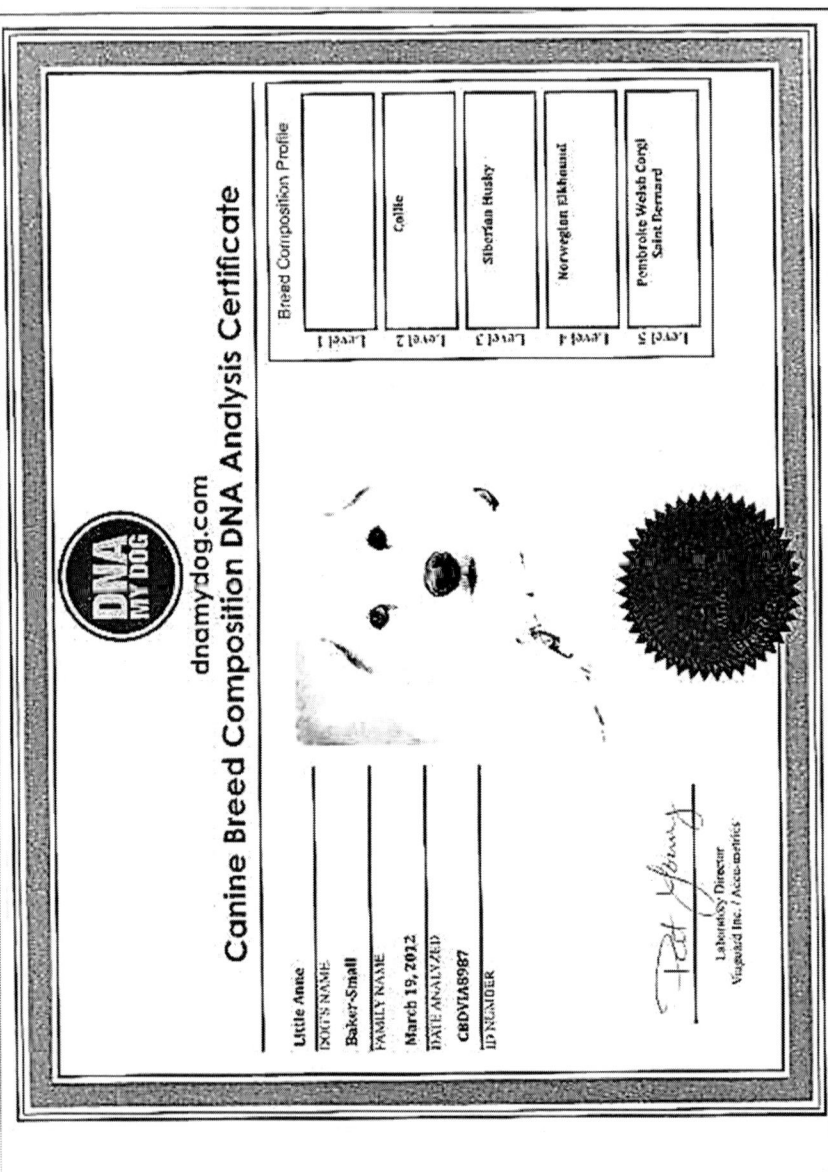

The end of May 2010, I received an email explaining the tragedy at Mile 26. I was heartbroken as I knew Jean-Eudes had been a great liaison between the Northern dogs and those of us down here that could help them. In this email, I along with many others was asked if I would be willing to help in any way. At that time a rescue was not organized and no one knew the horror that was unfolding. I of course replied that I had room for a dog……and the story begins.

As time went by, I heard nothing more about the Mile 26 dogs and my life went on as usual until I got a phone call, July 2nd I believe, asking if I could take one or two dogs. One dog was full of beans, loved people and seemed healthy. The other dog offered was in poor shape,

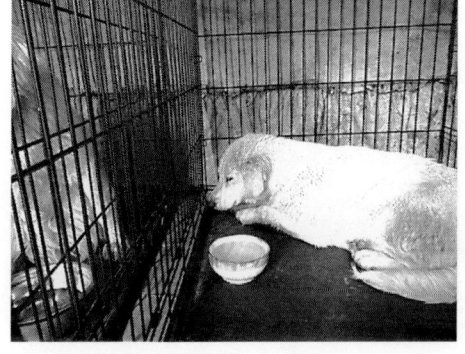

withdrawn and sickly. I explained that I had the knowledge and experience to deal with the worst of the two, so Little Anne was on her journey to me.

When she arrived, my first impression was, "Dear God…this poor little thing!" I was a little apprehensive as I didn't expect her to be as far gone as she was. She slunk under our car in the drive and shook. I tied a longer tether to her and walked away. We had company on this beautiful day and were sitting outside enjoying the sun. I kept a watchful eye on Little Anne as she lay there with wide black eyes, terrified. Approximately one half hour passed and suddenly the dirty little dog came slinking up onto our deck and lay down under my guests' chair. No one said a word, we continued our conversation.

Eventually my guest Bryan MacMillan reached down and began rubbing her neck. Little Anne took to the attention and fell sound asleep, a deep sleep that over the next few months caused me great concern. By that evening Little Anne began to feel safe and was following me everywhere. She had such a sweet, pretty little face and appeared to smile at me once in a while. I was falling in love. I still hadn't held her or really even stroked her but we were talking and that was a good thing. That night, upon going to bed, I realized just how badly she needed love.

I coaxed her into the spare bedroom where I planned to sleep with her for the time being and as I snuggled under the sheets Little Anne jumped up and curled up on my pillow, my head actually. It was right then that the ice was broken and real trust began. She snored and kicked and worst of all whimpered all night. Needless to say I didn't sleep well, but that was fine as it gave me time to touch her frail little body and realize just how sick she was.

Little Anne was one of the last few dogs to be rescued and had to endure the harsh reality that she was on her own. Although the ONR workers continued to drop food off at the site, bless their hearts, the remaining dogs had to fight each other, bears, wolves and the elements. Survival was difficult and becoming impossible for some like Little Anne.  She was rescued on June 30th, over a month after the fire and the death of her Master, a frail, weak little dog who was losing her will to live. She was found in her trap and carried into the loving arms of her rescuers by Anne and Max Kennedy, hence her name, Little Anne, named affectionately after Anne Kennedy. Anne wasn't sure if her little charge would make it at that time.

She was immediately brought to Iroquois Falls Vet Clinic to be health checked spayed and unfortunately dental work. Seven teeth were extracted from that tiny mouth. She was also pregnant and sadly due to her poor health, had to loose her three puppies.

When Little Anne came to me she was depressed and withdrawn, her coat was a filthy gray, her little face was deeply scared and her mouth swollen wide. She was skin and bones and full of worms. Her eyes were dull and full of fear. Three days after her arrival, I felt she trusted me enough to bath her and when I did, black soot poured out of her coat, but as hard as I tried, she didn't come clean but a white dog was emerging. Two days later I bathed her again and more soot poured out and sure enough, when the water flowed clear, a pure white dog emerged. She sparkled in the sun, she was so pretty!

As the days went by I began to worry as she would sleep an estimated twenty hours or more a day, not a normal dog sleep but a sleep so deep, I would put my hand on her chest to be sure she was still breathing, and she was but I was concerned. Periodically she would howl and cry in her sleep, such a mournful sound it would make me cry as I held her little sleeping head, wishing I could take those frightful memories away. A vet visit ensured me that she was fine and was probably sleeping off the stress, knowing she was safe and sleeping the best she had in perhaps her entire life. Time went by and she began to sleep more normal hours and not as deep. Her nightmares waned off too. Her energy level was on the rise and her  frisky personality was coming around. Every day, she became more of a clown.

We still had one more obstacle to overcome, Little Anne was afraid of  men and children. She would have nothing to do with my husband Gary or my son James. Gentle persuasion and frequent visits from kind strangers has helped her come around and now she loves almost everyone. She still has her reservations with some, and only she knows why, but it proves what love and patience can do. I was asked to foster this little dog and initially that was my plan, but as time went by, she and I became inseparable and my love grew into more than just love for a creature. I was in love with this dog. She was mine and I hers and it remains that way today and will until death parts us. This is one failure I am very happy to admit. (Foster failure)

Today, Little Anne is the picture of health and she glows from the inside out. Her bouncy personality is something we could only dream of a few years ago. Her strength and bravery inspired me to start a Facebook group called 'Little Anne's' Diamond Dogs, dedicated to rescue animals and the people who dedicate themselves to them. Needless to say, she dawns a diamond (rhinestone) collar representing the brave little princess she was born to be. An inspiration to all of us, the amazing dogs of Mile 26 have proven to be.

Thanks to the Northern Ontario Animal Welfare Society (NOAWS), Moosonee Puppy Rescue and the entire group of wonderful volunteers Little Anne's journey has led me to, who were involved in this dramatic rescue; a large beautiful group whom I love like family. A little white bush dog has changed my life forever and I will continue to be grateful to her for that. I know that some day I will have to live without her but she will live in my heart for eternity. My beautiful brave heart, my teacher, Little Anne. *Catherine Baker Small & family*

Little Anne's animal family includes Marti, Mitzi, Cooper, Maybe Cat, Petal the duck & Skittles the turtle.

Reflections of days past.....

Shylow

Hello;

I want to share Shylow's story with you. I first heard about the Mile 26 rescue/recovery from Sharron and Paul Purdy of Moosonee Puppy Rescue. Sharon had called me here in Haliburton and asked if I knew anyone that would be willing to foster some dogs that they and some volunteers were hoping to bring down to the Bracebridge area. I then called Margaret, the lady who boarded my dogs at the Dog House Boarding Kennel, and she immediately said she could foster four dogs.

I was then going to help transport them to Margaret by driving to Bracebridge and bringing down the crated dogs. I brought four dogs to Haliburton to be fostered that day, Shylow was one of them. I checked on them about a week later and Margaret said they were all doing well but Shylow. She just didn't seem to respond to anything or anybody. I went to visit them and she touched my soul as any one who has met these dogs, knows they can. I then discussed with my husband about bringing her home to our house. He of course felt that four dogs was going to be a little too much for me, but being the wonderful man he is, agreed to go and see her. Once he saw her, he knew she needed to be with us.

She came home and immediately bonded with our other three dogs and has been an absolute joy. Never had an accident in the house, chewed or gotten into garbage. She has never been anything but pure love in our lives. The vet feels she was about ten to twelve years of age at that time. We are blessed to have Shylow in our lives.

Kathryn and Gord Kidd

Shylow's pack mates Saul and T-Bone.

Lyra

Canine Breed Composition DNA Analysis Certificate

dnamydog.com

Breed Composition Profile

- Level 1:
- Level 2: Labrador Retriever
- Level 3:
- Level 4: German Shepherd Dog / Flat-Coated Retriever
- Level 5:

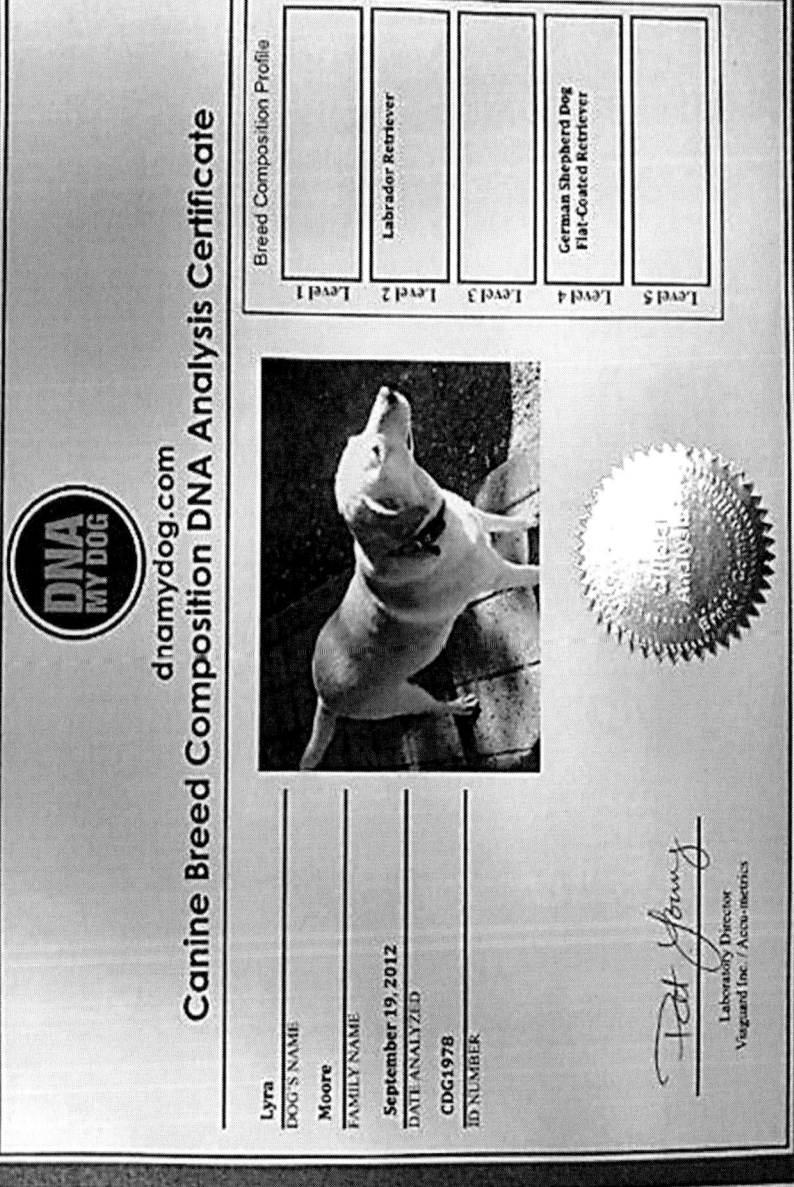

DOG'S NAME: Lyra
FAMILY NAME: Moore
DATE ANALYZED: September 19, 2012
ID NUMBER: CDG1978

Laboratory Director
Vagoard Inc. / Accu-metrics

After several years of my sons' requests for a dog, I decided in the fall of 2010 that the time was right for a doggie addition to our family. We thought about the kind of dog that would fit with our family and what we had to offer. After meeting a couple of dogs that I knew we were not the right family for, I talked to Jill at Pet Save in Lively. I spent some time telling her about my family, what we had to offer and what we were looking for. Finally she said, "I have just the right dog for you." We met Lyra and took her for a walk. She was beautiful, friendly and well behaved. Pet Save allowed us to agree to foster her for a few weeks, this gave us tome to check whether Lyra triggered any allergies (a serious concern) and to see how she got along with the rabbit members of our family.

After driving Lyra home from Pet Save, she tied to make a run for it when the car door was opened. I was terrified of Lyra bolting into the bush, so I jumped on top of her, pinning her to the ground and whacked my head on the car door. I could feel the goose egg swelling but was afraid to let Lyra go. I tried picking her up to carry her in the house but she would have none of that. Finally she figured out that it was at a stalemate and ended it by calmly standing up and walking into the house. For the first half hour she hid under the piano bench until we coaxed her out by scratching her ears. Once she discovered she could get her ears scratched just by sitting beside us, she decided that this was a pretty good place for her and she settled in.

The first night, Lyra decided she wanted to sleep on the sofa. Before bringing her home, I had laid down the rules for my kids, one of them was, no dog on the sofa. Lyra didn't get that message and she tried to slowly sneak her way onto the comfy chair by first resting her chin on the seat, then slowly one paw at a time. She was so cute that she convinced us to let her up on the sofa. She lounged there as if she'd been doing it her whole life. We nicknamed her Queen Lyra on her throne. Eventually we got her a nice doggy bed and reclaimed the sofa for ourselves. We suspect she still lounges there when nobody is around.

A few months after Lyra had settled into her new home on the first warm sunny day of spring, we all went for a walk through the bush just beyond our neighborhood. Lyra was especially excited; the ground was wet and muddy with many puddles to negotiate, but not Lyra. She aimed directly for every mud puddle along the path and then lay down in the puddle for a refreshing mud bath. We tried to keep her out of the mud but she seemed so happy we gave up and decided to let her wallow. After returning home we bathed her outside, it was a good day and no harm done, or so we thought.

The next morning Lyra greeted us in her usual way except her tail was pointing straight downward. Without a wagging tail she looked so sad yet she didn't seem sick, hurting, unhappy or frightened. It was as if her tail was broken, was that possible? I tried to find a vet, but it was Easter Monday and they were either closed or completely booked. I then turned to an internet search and found reference o Cold Water Tail Syndrome. A rare condition caused by exposure to cold water. The references assured me that it was temporary and painless. Sure enough in a few days Lyra had her wag back and looked like her usual happy self.

Lyra's favorite things include her evening walk around the neighborhood, ear scratches, group hugs, being the center of attention, Nathan's bed, large butcher bones, running through and rolling in fresh snow banks, rolling in the grass, running and jumping with her family, her dog bed, the back yard in the sun, middle of the kitchen during meal preparations and the sofa, when no one is home. She thinks we don't know but we've seen the evidence....

The best way to describe Lyra is in the words of her best friend, my son Nathan. "Lyra came to us from the Pet Save shelter in Lively. When we got her, she was really shy and rarely did anything except hide in the corner of our living room. She came out sometimes to get food but when we tried to take her out for walks, she could barely go up the street before panicking and running back home. That has changed a lot now. After she got to know us and the other people in the neighborhood, she's become a cheerful and playful dog. She's still calm and doesn't tear stuff up (thank goodness) but she loves to play. When we go outside, she runs around and prances about. During winter, Lyra runs around and stuffs herself into the snow and rolls on her back, looking desperate. There aren't many things that are impossible, but resisting to scratch her belly when she's like that is one of them. Lyra is also one of the most loyal dogs I've seen. She thinks my mom is the head of the 'pack' so she follows her everywhere! When we leave the house you can always see her with her poor desperate seeming puppy eyes looking out the window saying "Come back!" When we return, it's straight to the door with her. I love that dog."

Michelle, Charlotte and Nathan

Tara came into our lives in November of 2011 and she's finally found her forever home with us. When I first saw Tara, I knew she was a special dog. I saw that she was in need of a family who would love and cherish her and give her a good home.

Tara is the sweetest, gentlest dog I have ever met. She is right at home with her human pack. We can let her walk off leash and she will come right back for a treat and a pat. She chooses to spend most of her time outside and although she has some minor separation anxiety issues, she is a wonderful dog. We feel very privileged to have this special animal in our lives.

Tara is loving, trusting and loyal. She always looks forward to a belly rub, and she very much loves going along with the family for a car ride. Actually, she may go along with just about anyone in a vehicle, but we're working on that.

It has been an interesting journey, learning about Tara, a dog with such a special background and history. Tara has been loved by everyone whose life she has touched. The people responsible for her rescue and rehabilitation have had an enormous effect on her and on us. We are always learning about her quirks and her personality, and how well she fits in our lives.

Tara's history as a Mile 26 dog along with her difficulty finding her forever home makes us happy to offer her a peaceful, loving home with lots of exercise and praise for her good behavior. She has enriched our lives and will continue to do so as we will continue to offer her a stable and healthy home.

Dea Chute & Family

In June of 2010, our family dog of eleven years that we rescued from a shelter passed away. As a family, we decided that we wanted another dog, and that like the first, we wanted another rescue dog. We decided to look on the internet and came across a site called Petfinder. Through Petfinder we located a beautiful puppy called Whistle.

We soon learned that Whistle was from a litter of puppies that were rescued from the Mile 26 fire, just north of Cochrane Ontario. She survived because her brother Steamer (now Luke) helped get her to safety. Sharron from the Moosonee Puppy Rescue went up to Mile 26 to see what she could do to provide assistance. Sharron rescued the puppies that she could, including Whistle, and brought them back to Bracebridge.

After assessing Whistle, she was posted on Petfinder, and we contacted Sharron and filled out an application to adopt her. The story of Whistle and her siblings was truly sad, but we knew we could make a difference in her life by providing a loving home and all the attention that she would need to thrive and reach her full potential. Paul, Sharron's husband finally brought Whistle down for us to meet in Brampton on June 27, 2010. When we first met Whistle she was extremely nervous, but eagerly sniffed our home. She was only six pounds but already full of energy and ready to give and receive lots of love and attention.

She has been with us ever since and has been a wonderful addition to our family. She has grown to her full size now at thirty five pounds and has proven to be full of energy and has no fear when it comes to leaping off of steps and chasing soccer balls in our backyard. Each day she brings us more joy than the last, and we feel truly blessed to have found such a beautiful and vivacious dog.

Sal, Sue, Christina and Stephen Sapienza

We adopted Winnie on August 20, 2010 from the Clarington Animal Shelter at the age of seven weeks. We were overjoyed to be able to bring Winnie home the same day we met her. We wanted a female puppy and when Winnie was let out of the dog run, she came running to us. Earlier that same day, we had our laid our dog Holly put to rest and just couldn't think of going home without a puppy or a dog.

The Clarington Animal Shelter told us the story of how Winnie's mom Nellie and others were rescued from Mile 26. We knew we had an exceptional girl. Thanks to all the volunteers that have made it possible for us to have our Winnie. The Mile 26 dogs are truly special and anyone who is lucky enough to be owned by one understands why.

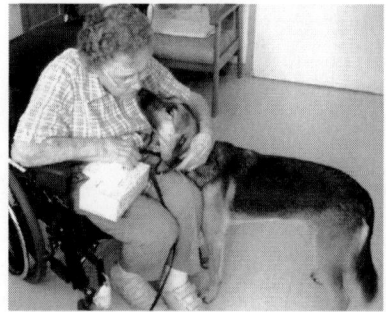

We take Winnie to the nursing home where my mother in law lives once a week. She has been visiting there since she came to live with us, and brings joy to the residents who live there. One lady asks "Where's Winnie" if we're running late, she can't wait to see her and get her kisses. After greeting her Grandma, Winnie just lies down and sleeps while we visit. (Sadly, Grandma passed on during the writing of this book, I'm sorry she won't see her little star here)

Early one morning last fall, Winnie alerted us to the meowing of a tiny kitten outside our front door. She kept barking until we got up and heard it too. Miss Kitty now lives with Winnie and her cat brother Eddie.

Winnie also sits in on Reiki courses that I teach and everyone loves her. She is a high energy girl and keeps us on our toes. Winnie gets lots of exercise and so do we. She loves to go for walks, car rides, play Frisbee, run, swim and chase squirrels.

Winnie's DNA revealed that she is part Siberian Husky, Doberman Pinscher, and Labrador Retriever. Winnie is a Mile 26 Special! She will continue to bring joy to everyone and always makes us and others smile with her "Oooooooo" noise that she makes. When Winnie is snuggled in bed with us, life is perfect.

Susan & Bill Rouse

The first time I saw a picture of a Mile 26 dog was on a friends Facebook page. His name was Papa, silly name I thought. His face had numerous scars, his ears looked mangled and damaged, but the soft sparkle in his eyes touched my heart.

There was no way I could even think of adopting him, I owned the dog hatingest dog ever! My Lab/Border Collie cross Sonnyboy, had ruled my house and life for the past fourteen years and he just would not tolerate another canine in his presence let alone his domain. Frankly, he believed he was a person and I loved my big gnarly dog and I wasn't about to make him uncomfortable.

Sonnyboy was 14, this would likely be, I felt in my heart, his last months. I often thought of Papa, wondering how he was doing and often mentioned him in the occasional prayer. I had heard through the grapevine that he had been adopted.

I had Papa's picture in my Facebook album, and recall being drawn to it, and sometimes would go online, look at him and wonder how he was doing.

Sonny passed away on March 16, 2012. Grief became my shadow, and that hollow place in my chest pained me. In late April, I received an email from a friend who volunteered her time at All Heart Pet Rescue. Papa was back and available for adoption. I rushed out to All Heart that day, and was able to take him home with me as a foster for a trial run.

He's not a normal dog they told me, this won't be easy, I was told. They were right, he is not a normal dog, he's an abnormally snuggly dog, an ankle clinger, cat chaser, deer stalker and painfully shy around people when I first got him. He was the complete opposite of Sonny; quite frankly, I hadn't expected this dog to be so different.

It's interesting how the different can become the familiar, and love can grow from little things. Like the way he curls up against me at night (epic pillow hogging aside) or his sappy gratitude for pieces of raw fish,

He loves the stuff! Papa has taught me there is room for a variety of different loves in our hearts; we just need to be willing to let love in.

It's been several months since I adopted Papa. He is not so shy with people he knows are friends of mine and greets them with a happy grin and wagging tail. He is empathetic and kind to children as long as they are gentle; he allows them to pet him. He knows all the dogs in our neighborhood and greets each with enthusiasm. He has gained confidence and courage, and is on a path of self discovery. I feel blessed to be a part of his journey.

Sincerely, Darlene

Proud Papa!

Papa's new pack mate Tank.

I see a wonderful journey ahead for you Papa...

In the summer of 2010, I had the pleasure to meet a small white dog named Little Anne when she was delivered to my neighbor Catherine Baker to be fostered. Upon meeting her, I was told the story about a heart breaking rescue that had occurred north of Cochrane Ontario at Mile 26 on the Ontario Northland Railway line. At this time I heard that there were other dogs that had been rescued at the same time as Little Anne, and that some of them were residing with Kathy Jeanneault at All Heart Pet Rescue in Powassan, ON.

As summer changed to fall, I began to realize how special this little white dog was. At this point, I decided to check out those other dogs at the shelter to see if there would be one there for me. I was introduced to Nellie and we hit it off right away. I proceeded to adopt her in early November and brought her home.

She was instantly accepted by my twelve year old Black Lab Jazz, which was very nice to see as he had been an only furchild for many years. Nellie became a part of the family right away and after about a week of adjustment soon became one of the most loving dogs I had ever met. She is always happy to see me when I walk in the door, full of kisses and constantly wanting to be close to me.

Then came word that a rescue group involved in the Mile 26 rescue, Northern Ontario Animal Welfare Society, were making a fund raising calendar featuring the Mile 26 dogs that had been saved in this dramatic rescue. I received one of those calendars from my good friend Catherine, and there in the month of November was a picture of my Nellie. In the same picture there was another dog named Kitchie. I found out that Kitchie was one of the younger dogs that had been a part of this rescue as well and had been a kennel mate of Nellie's at All Heart Pet Rescue.

It was now Christmas and with life being as hectic as it gets that time of year, I didn't think much more about it. After New Years, I was having so much fun with Nellie that I got thinking about seeing if I could adopt her kennel mate. I went to the shelter to meet Kitchie and instantly fell in love with her. She was a soft fur ball of life. I brought her home that day and as soon as we came in the door, Nellie greeted her

like the long lost pals they were, so happy to see each other. My black Lab was a little less receptive but over the next few days, even he started to accept Kitchie. Who wouldn't? Pretty soon they were all best friends, with Nellie & Kitchie wrestling non stop on the floor and the couch while my Lab watched like a big brother would.

We have been together now for over two years and they have been a wonderful addition to my family. Nellie is a very calm, quiet type companion while Kitchie is a bit of a wild child. Kitchie bounces around and teases me and the other dogs most of the time, always ready to run and play. I have enjoyed being a part of the Mile 26 Family and look forward to many more years of fun and frolics with these wonderful creatures. (Sadly Jazz passed during the writing of this book, and will be greatly missed).

Many thanks to the people involved in rescuing these animals, without you; I would never have had the pleasure of meeting these very special creatures.

Bryan MacMillan

In the summer of 2010 I was working at All Heart Pet Rescue, on summer co-placement while studying to become a Veterinarian Technician at Georgian College in Orillia. I first heard about the Mile 26 rescue from Kathy, in a discussion as to whether we could help despite our lack of space at the time. Knowing the situation of this rescue project, we decided we could take in seven to eight adult dogs.

It was quite late and dark when the truck pulled in, trailer of dogs in tow. I will never forget the sight of their seven little faces peering out from their kennels and knew right from the start that they were very special dogs. I got to help name them and we chose names that we felt not only suited them but many reflected their origins in Ontario. Nipigon, Abitibi (after the river they crossed on their journey) Papa, the old guy and patriarch, Moonshine (who would be a light in a time of darkness) and Dakota in memory of my recently deceased and beloved dog of fifteen years, and so on.

On their second day, we did a general physical exam on each of them and I started to gain their trust by hand feeding them and as time went on I spent more and more time out in the yard with them. Abitibi and Nellie were the first to try a leash walk, both balking at first but steadily improved, especially when walked together. After a few weeks, I started bringing Abitibi home with me at night. Abitibi showed strong separation anxiety and on one occasion chewed he way through a wooden door when I had left her for only about twenty minutes. I tried crate training her, but she managed to move the crate around the room and proceeded to chew ottomans, pillows and clothing. She certainly didn't care for confinement or being alone.

A second load of dogs soon arrived, including Gogama, Winkie, Albany, Kahuna (now Rocky) and Iceland (now Honey). Honey was quickly sent to another shelter as it appeared she may be pregnant. We later took in Tex from a shelter where he was having problems making progress. All of the Mile 26 dogs who came to us were timid and afraid, some were easy to win over, and others retreated deep inside a shell, avoiding any physical or eye contact. They needed time and patience to learn to love and trust. Before long, we had our suspicions that Moonbeam was pregnant. Sure enough, within days she produced one

sweet pup we named Moonshine. I often took her out in the yard where I would sing to her while Moonbeam followed, keeping a watchful eye on her puppy.

I started taking Abitibi home to Orillia with me on my days off, so she could become familiar with what would be her new home when I returned to school in the fall. She had become quite comfortable, brave and confident as time went by. One of her favorite buddies was Leggo. He had been severely injured at some point up at Mile 26 and was missing half of one front leg and most of one paw from the other front  leg. She still sees Leggo a few times a year and is still crazy about him.

In mid July I officially adopted Abitibi, although in my heart I had done it long before that. It took a few weeks for Abitibi to settle in when I returned to school, but with the destruction of a few minor household items and arguments over the use of a crate for her, all was soon well.

Just after Thanksgiving, I took in two foster kittens and named them Calvin and Hobbes. Abitibi was very curious and chased them around, but responded well to my 'gentle' command, and the kittens certainly loved her. Hobbes seemed to think she was his mom and Abitibi didn't mind, even to the point of Hobbes trying to nurse from her. At the end of the day, they were all cuddled together as a happy family, so Calvin and Hobbes were no longer fosters, but became permanent members of the family.

Abitibi is playful and affectionate, perhaps the most affectionate dog I've ever known. She has this uncanny ability to win over people, other dogs and even cats very quickly. Once she's won you over, she's in your lap giving kisses and her little tail wags constantly. I found I was being invited places just so I would bring Abitibi along!

I have had Abitibi in my life for almost three years and am thankful to have her. Watching her romping with one of her dog pals or splashing in the water, chasing squirrels up a tree trunk or snuggling with Calvin and Hobbes, gives me great joy.

Abitibi, (right) and one of her best pals Speckles, enjoying a brisk walk together.

Enjoying a day swimming.

To think of where she came from, to where she is now is mind boggling. My little dog was one of a pack of many, in a place with one human. Now she lives in a city with millions of people and accepts it all, including the dogs and people she greets as potential friends. She has accepted so many changes, taken them in stride and faced it all with her beautiful smile. When I think about it, there's a lot I can learn from this little dog, she is remarkable.

Barb Dingwall

When Schizzle arrived at Pet Save Lively shelter, she already had a room set aside for her and to this day it is called 'Schizzle's Room'. Shortly after her arrival, she gave birth to seven pups, just as beautiful as she is. These pups would have the luxury of being born in a warm and safe environment, and with Andrea Krats acting as mid-wife. They would not have to face a questionable fate being born in the harshness of Mile 26. It was reported she was a doting mom, and eventually all of her puppies were adopted within the Sudbury area. Unknown to Schizzle, someone nine hours away, had been watching the Mile 26 rescue from beginning to end as it unfolded on Facebook.

I have been involved in rescuing companion animals for over five years and have had considerable experience in training dogs over the past fifteen years, but now, finally retired am settled at home doing what I can by computer to assist rescues and fight for decent animal welfare. I also have a soft spot for senior dogs, and had recently adopted two, one of which I had just lost to illness. Sadly, cancer is the highest rated killer of canines.

I followed the Mile 26 rescue and was happy each time I saw another dog adopted out to a good home. Schizzle had become best friends with Frankie, another Mile 26 dog being housed at Pet Save. One day, Frankie's turn came, and he was adopted, leaving Schizzle alone with only her volunteer friends to comfort her. At this point in time, there were only five Mile 26 dogs still awaiting adoption, three at Pet Save and two at All Heart Rescue in Powassan. One of the Mile 26 group posted their photos on their Facebook page which prompted my call to Pet Save resulting in a two hour chat with Andrea Krats regarding adopting Schizzle. In my heart Schizzle was coming home and as news caught up on Facebook, her followers were ecstatic! I was already setting up Schizzle's very own Facebook page where we would post lots of photos and updates on her progress in her new home.

Schizzle had received other offers of adoption, but she was a big girl and stubborn at times. She did not take kindly to being man handled nor would she accept having children crawl on her. She is very beautiful, intelligent and has great potential to be a wonderful dog in the right hands.

Thankfully, the home and life I could offer was acceptable.

With all the arrangements made, finally on May 12, 2012, Andrea Krats and Sheelagh Johnson took Schizzle for her last walk at Pet Save before loading her in the vehicle which would bring her to her new home with me. She headed out with treats, dog food, some glucosamine chews to help seniors who may be a little arthritic, a 2011 calendar where she was Miss November, a DNA kit and hope for happy endings.

One test would be that she and Austin got along together. Austin who I had adopted eight months earlier, was a very old medium mixed breed dog, with little hearing left, glaucoma and very arthritic. I was outside walking Austin when the ladies arrived with Schizzle. My first thought was "Oh, what a big, beautiful dog!" She appeared much larger than what I was expecting. The sun jumped off of her beautiful rust colored coat, her fan like tail held high in the air. I took her lead and she walked along with Austin and I. Austin had a sweet nature and just wanted to be loved, so he was content. Schizzle was more concerned over where her Pet Save ladies were. After many bribes with treats of chicken tenders and a little urging, we got her inside the door where she immediately claimed the first bed found.

The first evening went well, and the following day, Mothers Day, was the official day of adoption. Schizzle was home! She would make the next leg of her life's journey here with me. I promised to make her life wonderful and after sharing a few tears, the girls left for their long drive back home, taking with them an invitation to visit any time in the future they wanted.

"Yes Schizzle, you're home!" As amazing as dogs are, and unlike human beings, they seem to live in the moment and relish each moment of life. Perhaps it's because their lives are so much shorter than ours. I have never been able to figure it out, but do believe in my heart that they know and sense love without it having to be spoken, also unlike human beings.

Schizzle enjoying a day at the lake.

Schizzle, Austin and I off for a walk.

I cannot say enough good words about Pet Save Lively. Had they not waited two years to find that 'right' home for Schizzle she would not be with me today. They knew the ins and outs of her personality and had the ability to read and understand her needs and wants. This is something that comes only when a great deal of time is spent with the dog. I will forever be indebted to Pet Save and all they have done for Schizzle and the others in their care. As a side note, Austin passed away peacefully three months later.

Schizzle is happy, goes for walks daily and travels in the car everywhere I go. She gets lots of comments on how beautiful and well behaved she is. Each night before bed, she gets as promised, kisses on her snout as I tell her, "This one is from Jill, this one from Andrea, one from Sheelagh and this one is from me!"

Caroline Coligan

I first became aware of the Mile 26 dogs through Georgian College, where I was in my second year of studies to become a veterinary technician. I had heard about them through the clinic, but at the time hadn't paid too much attention to it.

I met Winkie on my first Animal Care rotation which consists of taking care of assigned animals for a week. This includes their nutritional needs, exercise and medical requirements. I can't say, like everyone else that I instantly fell in love with Winkie, she was a great dog but was extremely quiet and didn't show much of her personality to me or the other students. By the end of my AC rotation, I began to spend more time with her and realized what a sweet dog she was. After my rotation was over, I found myself visiting her on my free time or just sitting in her kennel between classes, finding myself becoming more and more attached to her. The day she left the college, was the day I knew I had to adopt her.

Winkie the day she was rescued at Mile 26.

On November 5, 2010 I drove to All Heart Pet Rescue with a collar and leash, and was so excited to finally pick her up and bring her back to her forever home. I had played with the idea of changing her name, but after talking with Kathy and everyone that worked with her at the school, I knew I couldn't So, I made a slight adjustment. I wanted to keep the name given to her by the people who helped her, but also allow her to change and keep growing in her new life. So, Wink stuck!

I have never been so sure of the decision to adopt Wink, we are both so happy and I could never ask for a better dog. She is now playful, and an attentive dog with a personality that melts hearts. I find that she is a lot more outgoing and always wants to play with new dogs and loves to meet new people. Everyone she meets, whether a dog person or not, she can win over eventually.

I find there is such a big difference in her from the day we met a Georgian College to now. She is great with other dogs, people and we are working on cats. She now has a kitten friend named Hades that she loves to play and curl up with.

Wink has forever changed me and has helped me in so many ways I can't begin to describe. Being a student and now a young worker living away from my family, it is always nice to come home to someone who is happy to see me, no matter my moods. She is always ready to go for a run or swim or just lie on the couch and watch cat commercials (yes, those are her favorites) all day.

I know that everyone says they have the best dog, and they probably do. Wink suits my personality and lifestyle to a 'T' and although some days she drives me crazy, I could never picture my life without her. She reminds me that your past is your past but it also shapes the person you are today.

On a side note, I would like to thank all those who helped with her rescue and for writing this book. It means a lot to me to have her story shared and to have her here with me today.

Justine Campbell

We regularly visited the Clarington Animal Shelter as we wanted a new addition to our family. We had been looking for about a year. I had lost my dog Luckie, also a stray, due to old age, and I really missed her. We also have another dog named Diesel, that we had adopted twelve years before,, but he is more my husbands dog, and I needed my girl. The timing had to be right, with two young boys, I knew it would take a lot of time, patience and love, but finally decided we were ready!

We put in an adoption application in the spring of 2010, and in the summer, received a call from Karen at Clarington, that the first Mile 26 litter had been born. We were heading out on vacation and not wanting to leave a new pup with family, but were told that there was a second litter due around the first of September. Perfect!

The call came, and Karen asked if we were still interested in a puppy. Our oldest son was gone for the first day back at school and our youngest was at home. We were in the car & on our way in no time. When we arrived at the shelter, we were taken to the big cage where the puppies were.

Sophia (Mile 26 Clute) had been taken elsewhere at the shelter for some rest. Being a mom again was taking its toll on her. She was getting older, had been through so much and was exhausted. We were told she was a very loving and protective mother.

I wanted a female pup, there were some bigger ones, then there was the runt! Cocco! I picked her up and sat with her in the chair. She kissed me like crazy, as I looked in my husbands' eyes; I knew she was mine already. They offered to clean her up, give her a microchip and we could come back for her in a few hours. We took the time to shop for 'puppy' things then raced back, arriving just as they were finishing her up.

Our oldest son Owen, still at school, had no idea what was going on. When we picked him up from school, and as he jumped up into his seat, Cocco caught his eye. I think she took his breath away and he didn't know whether to smile or cry. That moment was priceless. Owen had been asking for another dog for some time, he seems to share a special bond with them.

As Cocco grew, she also grew to love our other dog Diesel. She pampers him like crazy, cleaning and giving him dental check-ups! He doesn't have the energy to play too much, but will play tug of war. This involves her pulling him around on his side at the end of a chew toy. Diesel puts up with her and I'm sure deep down, he loves her too.

Cocco's first CIBC walk for cancer. Diesel teaches Cocco the ropes.

From day one, she has been my shadow. I would walk her off leash on the trails. I often looked back for her, only to find her right at my feet. Now when we walk, she is never more than about twelve feet away, or without looking to ensure I'm there. I often look back at my three 'children', my boys on either side with Cocco in the middle.

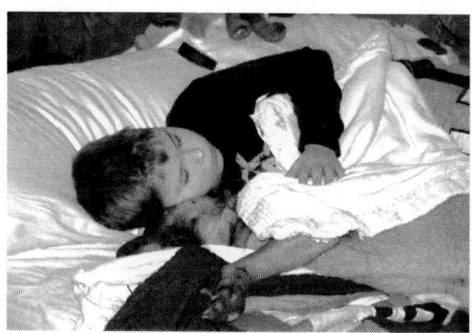

Owen suffers from sleep anxiety and has a hard time sleeping by himself at night as well as general worries that at times consume him. Besides us, his parents, offering him the love and support he needs, our older dog Diesel to whom he was very bonded, slept by his side offering comfort and security through his difficult nights. Now Cocco was happily taking over that job, giving Diesel some help in his old age. She seems to support all that we need, and joins us every year in our walk as a family supporting the CIBC fund raiser for cancer.

Cocco tends to be a bit nervous, is fearful of the vacuum and motorized sounds. She is very aware and cautious of her surroundings. She is very submissive with strangers and seeks approval. Once she gets over that, she is fine. She has endless energy and loves to play fetch. She is very intense and concentrated in retrieving that ball. She is very good with our cat, always nibbling on him wanting to play. I cannot imagine her being born and raised at Mile 26. It was only recently that we learned of her background. It was not disclosed when we adopted her. We were just told that the 'moms' were picked up, perhaps they were fearful that her background might make people think twice about adopting the pups. I feel so badly for all of those dogs, especially the ones left behind. I can say that Cocco has been the perfect addition to our home, right down to bringing us her food or water dish if she finds them empty. Her ability to communicate with us is really neat. These are not tricks, she has come by them on her own. She is very intelligent. Finding out where Cocco comes from has made us appreciate her that much more, and I wish more could have been saved. So sad that some turned their backs on them, those who didn't are heroes in our eyes.

Thanks for letting us share Cocco's story.

Shawn, Denise, Owen and Keenan Cochrane

Canine Breed Composition DNA Analysis Certificate

dnamydog.com

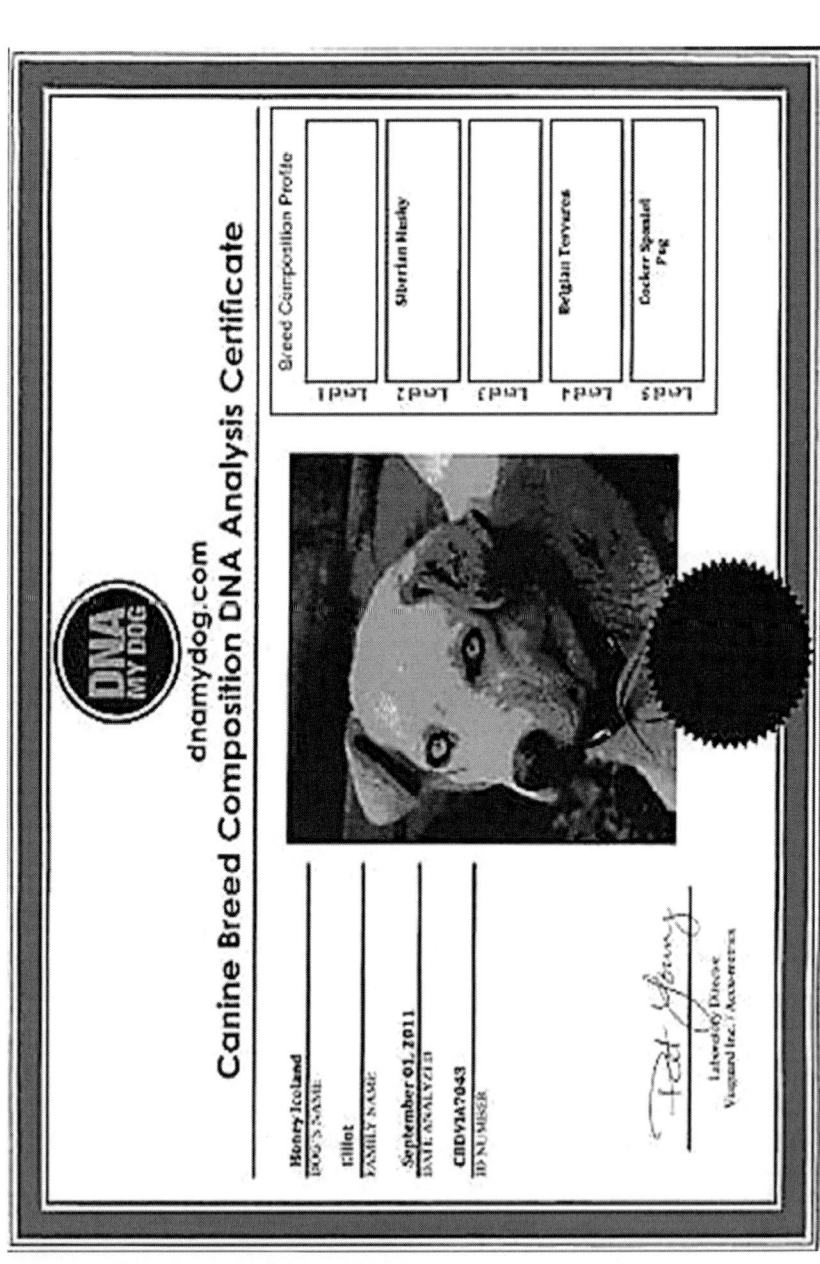

Breed Composition Profile

- Lvl 1:
- Lvl 2: Siberian Husky
- Lvl 3:
- Lvl 4: Belgian Tervuren
- Lvl 5: Cocker Spaniel / Pug

DOG'S NAME: Henry/Iceland
FAMILY NAME: Elliot
DATE ANALYZED: September 01, 2011
ID NUMBER: CBDV1A7043

Laboratory Director
Vetgen Inc. / Ann Arbor

Canine Breed Composition DNA Analysis Certificate

dnamydog.com

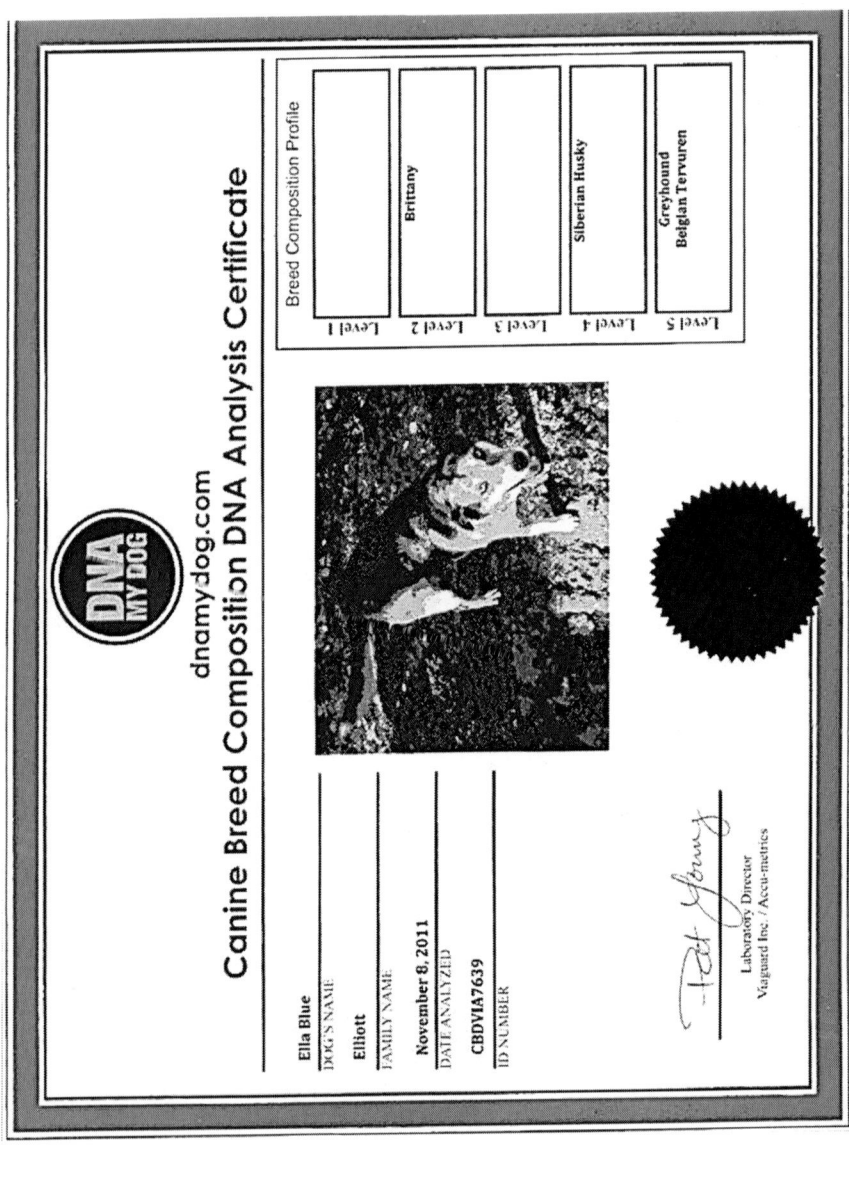

Breed Composition Profile

Level 1	
Level 2	Brittany
Level 3	
Level 4	Siberian Husky
Level 5	Greyhound / Belgian Tervuren

DOG'S NAME: Ella Blue
FAMILY NAME: Elliott
DATE ANALYZED: November 8, 2011
ID NUMBER: CBDVIA7639

Laboratory Director
Vaxguard Inc / Accu-metrics

I became aware of the homeless dogs and their situation at Mile 26 while watching MCTV news while our family was having supper. The images of the wet dogs, looking so forlorn and eager for human attention was a heart wrenching sight. A day or two later there was an article in the local newspaper about the dogs at Mile 26, with a plea from local rescues for volunteers and supplies. The article also referred to a Mile 26 Facebook page which I immediately joined to follow the story. At this time I donated monetarily to the Northern Ontario Animal Welfare Society as this group had taken the lead on this rescue.

I convinced my husband that it would be a good thing to foster one of these dogs, but had to be very selective due to the strong probably they would have a strong prey drive for smaller critters, and we have two cats. A dog named Iceland was posted on the Facebook page that appeared to be a blonde husky/lab mix with hauntingly blue eyes. I eventually tracked her down and learned she was being fostered in the Toronto are as she did not do well in a shelter facility. Buy now I had fallen completely in love with her and my fostering idea had turned into an adoption plan. I was thrilled when my husband agreed and I began corresponding with the Moosonee Puppy Rescue expressing my interest. Her foster mom was working on some behavioral issues, but they would decide when the time was right and in Honey's (her new name) best interest for a successful adoption.

In late July of 2010, Honey escaped her foster home. A bush dog on her own in a huge city! I was so relieved when I heard she was reunited with her foster mom in a matter of three days. Eventually Honey was spayed, our adoption approved and on August 28, 2010 my son, husband and I headed off on a long drive to pick up Honey just south of North Bay. When we arrived, the image I saw will remain with me forever. It was one of a small, frightened shell of a dog. I wanted to give her an awesome life and show her that the world really wasn't a bad place and she could live life the way a loved and domesticated dog should. I silently vowed I would for as long as she lived.

For the next five months, we watched an amazing journey as she started to come out of her shell. She spent most of her time avoiding open spaces, often scattering to hide at the slightest noise. She thrived on routine, and suffered great anxiety over any changes. She would refuse to eat or throw up. Honey often had a look in her eyes like she was deep in thought a million miles away. We did all we could to offer her calm surroundings, a place she could feel safe. There were many times I felt her progress was slow, but received lots of support through the Save The Dogs at Mile 26 Facebook page, seeing others who had these dogs were having issues of their own. Unless you had one of the rescues from Mile 26, you could never understand. They are indeed unique in their behaviors, and I believe this made them even more loveable.

Honey is still slowly evolving from her wild instincts and learning that man is not the enemy. Honey is afraid of all people outside of her immediate family. She does however love to meet other dogs and dances up to them making the sweetest little grunts and whines. I cannot and likely will never be able to walk her in public places. I accept that and it's not an issue for me. Whether it's genetics or from a previous tragedy, I will never force her to endure stress or anxiety.

Honey's favorite thing is water! Puddles, creeks, lakes, swamps, dirty and muddy or not, she loves to get wet. I definitely see her smile and her behavior is that of a happy confident girl when we walk the trails in the bush.

Ella Blue, another Mile 26 rescue dog with hauntingly blue eyes, joined our family on September 21, 2011. She was one of the three I had originally taken an interest in after the rescue. Ella Blue had also escaped from those trying to care for her, only this time; it took three months for her to be finally captured. I wanted her in our home, but knew in my heart that it was not a good idea to bring a third dog in, with our original dog Roxy and while we still worked with Honey's issues. I did however continue checking in on her through the Timmins Humane Society's website and was thrilled to find her adopted in December. Occasionally after that, I would still check in, perhaps intuition was telling me I should, and on September 16, 2011, my worst fear happened. Ella Blues' picture appeared as back up for adoption.

I posted her information on a new Facebook page that included many familiar with the Mile 26 dogs and their story, hoping to find that special home with people who would understand her needs. I was struggling with my conscience and concerned that Ella Blue may end up in the wrong home, misunderstood or worse, euthanized. With overwhelming feelings, I completed an adoption form, was accepted and spent the rest of the day in a bundle of nerves. How was I going to explain this to my husband who was adamant of not having a three dog family? I finally told him and that I would be picking her up the next day. It all worked out, as I guessed he realized just how serious this was and something I had to do. The Human Society manager arrived, and there was Ella Blue. I was so emotional and felt like crying. The feeling was surreal. She has those big ice blue eyes that look deep into your soul. She was not a

fearful dog like Honey, but a trusting, receptive, totally submissive little girl. I was smitten, as Ella Blue laid her head on my lap as we headed home. Once home, they all checked each other over, and other than a few low growls from Honey, all went well. I didn't see any sign that they remembered one another, despite having gone through hell together just over a year before up at Mile 26.

Ella Blue is a charmer. Quiet, obedient, submissive and excellent on a leash, she fit right in with my family like she had been there forever. She loves people, is an awesome cuddler and loves attention from anyone. Judging by her behavior, I think she must likely have been one of Jean-Eudes favorites and one of the top dogs in the pack. It didn't take long for my husband and son to fall for her. My son was thrilled when I told him Ella Blue could sleep in his room.

At the point of writing this, we haven't had Ella Blue for very long, but we believe she is pretty much an open book with few surprises. She enjoys our daily hikes along the trails without her leash, has good recall and loves to be rewarded with treats. She, like many other Mile 26 dogs, has terrible teeth which we will have to monitor. She is very food driven but is slowly learning not to be a table food beggar, and should shed some extra weight. We're working it all out and she'll get it. After all, she is not a stupid girl, She is a survivor!

I feel so blessed that I have made a difference in their lives, and they have definitely made a difference in mine. I can relate to many of their feelings on so many levels. I am forever thankful Honey now feels safe with me and I do believe we are given the dogs we need. Each of these special dogs learned how to survive the best way they could and it will be something that stays with them forever.

Susan Elliott

Roxy and Ella Blue

Roxy and Honey

Ella Blue

Honey

Our beautiful Mile 26 girls Ella Blue and Honey

There are many wonderful success stories that have come out of this rescue, and these stories have to be told. But part of the success of these dogs is overcoming what they had to endure. I think the whole story needs to be told. Life at Mile 26 before the fire (both the good and the bad), the tragedy and trauma of the fire, the rescue and the life of the dogs now.

I have often said, long before Mile 26, that if I didn't keep myself in check, I could easily end up as the guy with two hundred dogs. I don't want to get to this point because I know having that many dogs leads to most of them being neglected. They're just not getting the care they need. It's better for both me and the dogs if I were to limit my pack to just a few and give each the care they need and deserve. I think the Dogman was a kind man and well intentioned. Reading the whole story will likely prevent someone else from taking in one too many dogs. Remember the quote: *"Those who forget history are doomed to repeat it."*

Note*

Sadly, Leggo received a severe injury at some point in his life where he lost half of his left leg and half of his right paw. This photo was taken at the Mile 26 rescue sight. I find it remarkable that Leggo survived the years he did, as he was not physically capable to easily make a swift retreat from danger or fight off an attack from any sizeable animal. Being the bonded pack these dogs were, I can only assume he had the protection of the pack or Jean-Eudes who took him under their wing. I had the extreme pleasure of meeting Leggo and his family at the walk-a-thon for All Heart in 2012. What a personable and happy fella he is!

We adopted Leggo on October 25, 2011. When we first got him, we were trying to get to know him. I wanted to know if he liked to play, and picked up a stick to see if he would show some interest in chasing it. As soon as he saw it, he showed a definite fear. Was he beaten at Mile 26? I don't think so! Jean-Eudes was a dog lover and I can't picture him beating any dog. Leggo's fear has to come from another source. A short while later, we got our first snowfall of the season. As soon as I picked up the shovel, Leggo hunkered down and scampered in absolute fear. I came to realize that it is shovels he fears and anything similar: broom, mop, stick. I have spent a lot of time desensitizing him to this fear to where I can now place it next to him if necessary and he trusts my good intentions, although I avoid it when I can since I don't want to scare him.

It was mentioned that the Dogman would euthanize the males in an effort of population control. I heard or read of this somewhere but I can't find the reference. It is not my intention to make Jean look bad or cruel. I'm sure he took no satisfaction in having to do this, but with the resources he had, did what he had to do in taking care of this huge pack of dogs and in the best way he could. I believe Leggo was a failed attempt. He was taken pity on out of his love for the dogs, bandaged up and kept safe as a house dog. I understand these thoughts are not pleasant ones, but I also believe it brings in to focus, the harsh and sad realities of life for all who inhabited Mile 26. It also brings out an even greater admiration, respect and understanding of these dogs and their often odd behavior in adjusting to such a new and different way of life.

Leggo lives a good life now, safe, loved and no doubt spoiled. I hope your book has a long chapter reserved for the wonderful people who handled the dogs on their journey to our homes. The various shelters who took them in, for the most part sight unseen. Kudos also to the ONR executives and employees who so generously offered many services to the rescuers. Without them, this rescue would not have been possible. On Leggo's behalf, we send many thanks to Kathy at All Heart and the many others who deserve to share the spotlight!

From Gaby;

Hi all and I have a special story to share about my little buddy Leggo. When we adopted Leggo, I didn't realize then just how much this little *white dog would affect my life. In the following year, I lost my best friend who had died peacefully in her sleep on October 29, 2011. I cannot say how much I was devastated by her loss.*

Leggo seemed to know how much I was hurting and this little guy, even tho' he has suffered in his life was my hero. He cuddled me, sat beside me in his own way and consoled me like no one else could. This little trooper stood by me with a love that was unconditional and sensed that I needed him beside me. He usually does sleep on our bed, but for a time, was always there, cuddled up beside me offering his love quietly and patiently. When it was especially rough, he was right there for me to pet him and stayed until I was OK. Then, it was off to his favorite couch but always returning if he sensed I needed him. Leggo is my little buddy and I am so grateful he came into my life. I know he is not a person but animals do feel emotion and can be the best thing for one who is hurting. I know, because Leggo was there for me. The Mile 26 dogs are so special because even through adversity, they are the best animals at being the most faithful pets one could ever need. That is my story, sounds mushy, but so very true for me.

Gille Giroux and Gaby Messier

Leggo meets Bandit, his new pack mate.   *Leggo loves the squirrels.*

Just chillin'   *With Kathy at All Heart Rescue*

Leggo goes swimming!   *Leggo just being Leggo*

Canine Breed Composition DNA Analysis Certificate

dnamydog.com

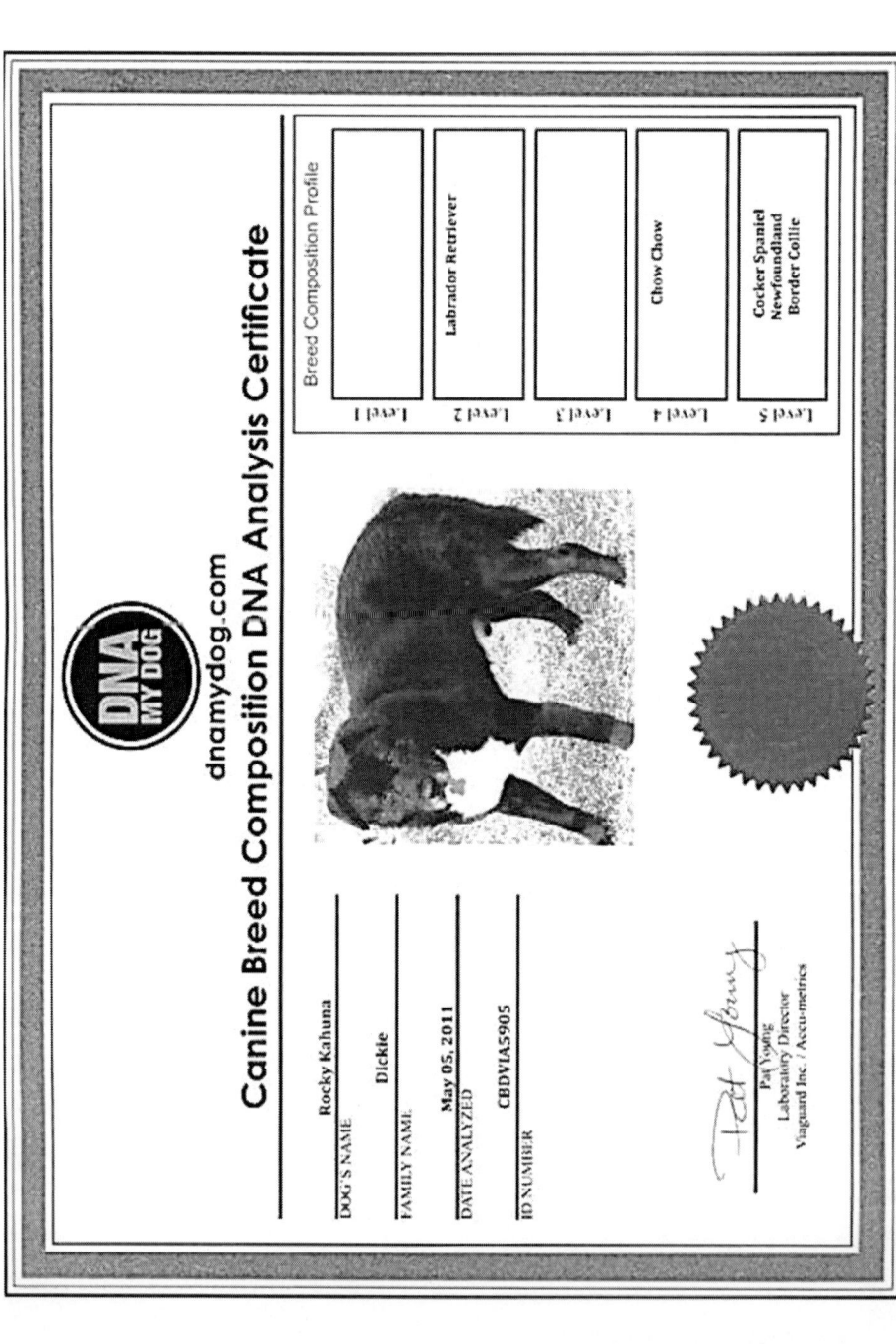

DOG'S NAME Rocky Kahuna
FAMILY NAME Dickie
DATE ANALYZED May 05, 2011
ID NUMBER CBDVIA5905

Pat Young
Laboratory Director
Vanguard Inc. / Accu-metrics

Breed Composition Profile

Level 1	Level 2	Level 3	Level 4	Level 5
	Labrador Retriever		Chow Chow	Cocker Spaniel Newfoundland Border Collie

We had just put the news on TV one day in mid August of 2010 as they announced they would be showing a very touching video of a large dog rescue currently taking place near Cochrane Ontario. Being the animal lovers we are, we sat glued to our chairs waiting to see what was going on. When they started to roll the video, we were very emotionally moved by what we saw and heard regarding these poor dogs. At the end of the video, a Facebook page was given where the public could go and find out what they could do to help if they chose to get involved. That is where I saw the photo of a dog named Kahuna (now Rocky), who instantly attached himself to my heart. Rocky's cover picture was made using that photo.

Looking into those eyes and the story I saw in them was overwhelming. As I went through the Facebook page, it was obvious that these people were doing an outstanding thing and needed all of the support they could get. Although I have read of other rescues and terrible plights of animals in need, this rescue became the first thing I checked on in the morning and the last at night, not to mention several times through every day for weeks. At some point in October, I felt I had to find out where this dog was and how he was coping. I asked this on the Facebook page and was responded to by three lovely ladies, Catherine, Anne and Carla, two of whom were active volunteers at the rescue sight through the Northern Ontario Animal Welfare Society.

I was informed that Kahuna was in the care of All Heart Pet Rescue in Powassan, and given the phone number, email address and Facebook page information. Over time, these three ladies became friends who I am grateful to every day since, for responding the way they did that first day. They confirmed that no, I wasn't really crazy as I explained my heart felt an obsession to find this dog and bring him home. They offered to help that happen in whatever way they could. We were on a mission to fulfill my dream if it was meant to be.

I spoke with Kathy at All Heart about Kahuna and she was very forthright about his condition. He was not doing well adjusting in his new situation and was going to take what she felt was quite some time to come out of the deep shell he had buried himself in and join the land of the living again. Aside from obvious visible scars from his past life, he was heavily scarred on the inside too. I was welcome to stay in touch and obtain updates as to his progress.

Without going into great detail, Kahuna's journey proved to be a long one. By early February of 2011 he was finally making baby steps toward his new world. Over the months past, Kathy and I had become well acquainted with each other, and my goal of a trial adoption approved for when he was ready. I was kept up on his every improvement and starting to feel like I already knew him very well. I was now even more dedicated to bringing this boy in to our family and had no doubt it would happen. Early February, I had the idea that if I sent a care package for Kahuna, he would somehow know that he had a family waiting for him and that he needed to get this done in order to come home. I found a big soft teddy bear and packed it in a box along with a few stuffed toys, treats , a blanket and my favorite old sweat shirt hoping he would feel the love thru the scent of family that went along in that box. We don't know if it was coincidence or maybe there was a little magic involved, but when Kathy opened that box with Kahuna, and even put my old sweat shirt on him, things seemed to take a turn for the better. He started to show an interest in things around him and one morning as I checked in to Facebook, there was a post from Kathy and so many happy responses to this big announcement. There was Kahuna, head up and eyes focused, standing in Kathy's office! This was the dog who so recently wouldn't even step out of his kennel on his own.

From this day on, it was all up hill. He was finally in a good enough physical and mental state to have a badly infected tooth repaired and be neutered. Kathy stayed with him for hours through his first night with his teddy bear by his side while he slowly recovered from a very long day of surgery. The phone call from her the next day relieved all of our worries; he was going to be just fine! We set a date of March 17th as the big day for us to come up with our other two dogs and bring Kahuna home. Being of Irish decent, I thought St. Patrick's Day was the perfect timing to bless our trial adoption with good luck.

Getting through those next weeks seemed like an eternity. We had waited so many months already but the days now were dragging. Finally the big day came! Teeka and Nub were loaded in the truck and we hit the road for Powassan at seven am. Our friends Catherine & Gary Small, and Bryan MacMillan, who we had met through Facebook and Mile 26, were going to meet us for the first time at the rescue. So much excitement to look forward to! We arrived around 10:30 am and were greeted by all of them up near the office. Everyone held a camera including Catherine's son James. Seems I wasn't so nuts after all, we shared the same emotions of that day. Kahuna was going home after nine long months of patient rehabilitation. I don't think I need to say much more, other than it felt more like a long awaited reunion the first time I got to put my arms around that dog. We had been kindred souls for some time already, just waiting for that day.

Kahuna has continued to grow and blossom from the day he arrived home. He has gone from a dog I fed by hand in a closed room to the first one in the kitchen at meal time. The months of deep sleeps and nightmares have also passed. His head is held high and his tail always up and wagging. To strangers, he appears somewhat quiet and maybe a little sad, but we see his smiles and his attempts at play when it's just us together. Like the others, he needs a stable daily agenda and order of things. He does not adapt well to changes in routine, but accepts it in time. He is forever by my side, just where he is supposed to be, displaying the truism that despite the torn raggy ears and battle scars, there is always hope no matter how dark the path to attain a goal may be. He is our Rocky now (eye of the tiger), and has completed our little family like nothing else could. Did I mention how much "I love this dog?"

Terry & Marilyn Dickie

Working at All Heart with Kathy
Nellie & Kitchie and Bryan

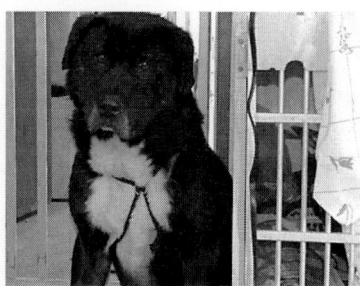

The day the light came on.

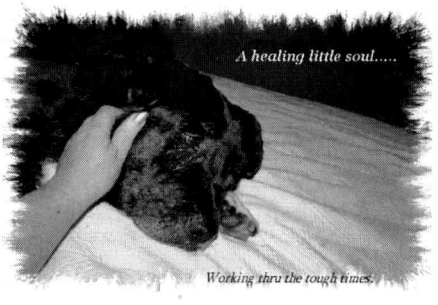

Afterword

Well, thus ends telling the story of the rescue at Mile 26 in 2010, but as long as these dogs and their new generation are with us, those families blessed with them will continue to spread the word of their amazing survival against the odds. Now shared in print, their inspirational story will never die. Long after they are gone, what they brought to those who loved them will continue as an inspiration of how together we can make a difference.

In a world that often appears to be running amuck, stories like this restore my faith that there is still hope as long as there is a priority to help those who can't help themselves. That in my world is the animals. I hope those reading this will include them in their passion to do some good in their lives. In this world, we are their only voice and hope.

The whole venture of this rescue story becoming a book, started with one Mile 26 mom's suggestion in 2011 of trying to track down where all of the adopted Mile 26 rescue dogs ended up. From there I could see the dream for our special dogs to make a huge contribution to animal welfare through us lending them our voice to share their journey. I now understand fully why that sad, black dog named Kahuna I saw posted on Facebook, gripped my heart so firmly and became a huge part of my life. What a source of comfort, pride, admiration and inspiration he and all the others have been, and will continue to be.

It took well over a year of searching to find the families we did, and over another year to put as many pieces together as possible and form the making of a book. It was a heart felt group effort by the Mile 26 families, rescues and volunteers that chose to be a part of it all. We had a dream, and along with that dream has come multiple friendships made across the many miles of Ontario and as far as the Maritimes with the family of the single little puppy born at All Heart Pet Rescue. We, because of the shared love and compassion for a special group of rescuers and dogs, were brought together as one huge family whose common desire is to raise awareness of the needs of our animals. The fulfillment of that dream will be the ability of providing funds to support these animal rescues and shelters to continue the good work they do for our animals in need.

In closing, I would like to add to memory, the names of four beautiful dogs that sadly passed shortly after the rescue. Their journey is just as important, they are just as loved, and will never be forgotten. *Gogama, Moe, Big Mama* and *Chesco* are the ones I can confirm are no longer with us. Perhaps it was meant to be that way. Their fate decided by a wisdom and power greater than we. I like to believe their spirits have joined the Dogman and the other members of their pack who now run forever free at Mile 26.

To the Mile 26 Dogs, thank you for making the journey home.

Out of suffering have emerged the strongest souls. The most massive characters are seared with scars.

Khalil Gibran

Order Form

Want to order more copies? It's easy, this is how!

Book price is $20.00 + shipping   *(All orders are sent thru Canada Post)*

Please email your order to: withhopetheywaited@hotmail.com

**If you do not have email available, orders can be mailed (please include your phone number) to 'With Hope They Waited', Box 63, Apsley, ON K0L 1A0 or call 705-775-3001
**Orders by email preferred.*

Please include all of the following information.

The number of copies you are requesting.

Your name and complete mailing address.

Your method of payment.

* *Payment can be made by cheque or Interac e-Transfer*

When your email is received, you will receive a response within 24 hours, advising you of the amount due ($20.00 per book + shipping cost) and expected date of shipping. Once your order is confirmed, you will receive your order number along with instructions for payment by 'e-transfer' if that is your choice for payment.

Thank you for supporting our animal rescues!

ISBN: 978-1-77084-328-8